HARDEN'S

London
for Free

Research Manager: Antonia Russell
Additional research by Shari Margolin

© Harden's Limited, 2001

ISBN 1-873721-41-2

British Library Cataloguing-in-Publication data:
a catalogue record for this book is available from
the British Library.

Printed and bound in Finland by
WS Bookwell Ltd

Harden's Limited
14 Buckingham Street
London WC2N 6DF

Distributed in the United States of America by
Seven Hills Book Distributors,
1531 Tremont Street, Cincinnatti OH45214

Contents

Introduction

What can you do in London for free?

World-famous parks, beautiful ancient woodlands, great museums and galleries, spectacular annual events and superb entertainments – the capital has an unrivalled range of free attractions.

As you will see, whatever your age and interests, whether you're a parent with children to entertain, a Londoner wanting to explore or a visitor to this great city, you really can do a lot of wonderful things here without paying a penny.

Is everything in this book really absolutely free?

Yes. Except where clearly stated to the contrary, everything in this book is free of charge. The only qualification is that if an asterisk (*) appears next to a name this means that free access is restricted in some way. The attraction may be free only at certain times (in which case the times we give in the small print are only those when there is no charge), or, in a few cases, you may not have access to the whole building. Many of the capital's larger, free-access museums and galleries also have regular, additional exhibitions for which there is a charge.

Just in case there is any confusion, where shops, markets, pubs or cafés are mentioned, they are included because they offer great window-shopping opportunities or because we thought it would be helpful for you to know about them. Sadly, there's a charge for the goods and services they offer.

Transport (Shanks's pony aside) also must be paid for. We would recommend any visitor to buy a Transport for London Travelcard – they are very good value and once you have one you can zip around the capital with no regard to expense. Daily Travelcards can be bought after 9.30am and, subject to zone restrictions, allow unlimited transport on buses, tubes, Docklands Light Railway and Tramlink trains.

Organisation

How is the book laid out?

First, geographically. We've split London into six areas, starting with Central (which is mainly the area usually called the West End). The next three are West (starting at Hyde Park), North (starting at Regents Park) and South (including everything south of the river). Going eastwards, we've subdivided the world into The City (EC postcodes) and The East End (E postcodes). Map references are given, where applicable, after the telephone number.

Secondly, as in England everything depends on the weather, we've divided each of the above sections into outdoor and indoor attractions. The introduction to each chapter summarises the highlights of the area concerned and tells you where you can get further local information. In addition, we've suggested sightseeing walks in most areas, to help you get your bearings, and to join up the various free attractions in the vicinity.

We have given the most up-to-date information available, but details change and it's always a good idea to call ahead (or look at websites, where applicable) to check opening times and any other details of particular interest. If you are making a special trip, you should always confirm the arrangements that apply over holiday periods – opening hours may be modified, of course, but there may also be special events worth knowing about.

Indexes

If you're interested in a particular type of attraction, wherever it is to be found, don't miss the indexes. There, we've given lists of all the museums, all the parks, all the galleries, and so on, to make sure you don't miss out on anything.

We hope that this book will help you to find London as fascinating a place as we continually do. And if you find something we've missed, please do write to tell us.

Richard Harden   **Peter Harden**

Londonwide
information

Introduction

A huge amount of free information about London is there for the taking. It's very difficult to find yourself far from a public library, and you don't of course need to be a resident of the area concerned to go and browse through the newspapers, listings magazines and guide books.

The most central comprehensive institutions are:

Westminster Reference Library
(35 St Martin's Street WC2, (020) 7641 4636)

Victoria
(160 Buckingham Palace Road SW1, (020) 7641 4287)

Chelsea
(Old Town Hall, King's Road SW3, (020) 7352 6056)

St Pancras
(opposite the railway station NW1, (020) 7974 5833)

Swiss Cottage
(88 Avenue Road NW3, (020) 7974 6522)

Consult the telephone directory to find out where your local library is (listed under the name of the relevant borough).

Westminster Reference Library, just by Leicester Square also offers an opportunity to search the world wide web free of charge. Bookings are taken in advance and you are limited to an hour's use at any one time. Understandably it's very popular. Bookings: (020) 7641 4636. (Times: Mon-Fri 10am-8pm, Sat 10am-5pm)

Libraries are also great places to find posters and leaflets about what's going on in an area, so if you want inspiration for free things to do close to home, your local library is almost certainly the best place to start.

Locals shouldn't overlook the tourist information offices, which often have a lot of information about events that are of just as much interest to Londoners as they are to visitors. In each of the area chapters, we've listed these offices.

The following services provide information on a pan-London basis.

London Tourist Board SW1

Victoria Station   2–4B

The main Tourist Information Centre of the LTB at Victoria Station welcomes millions of visitors every year. As a general source of free, up-to-date information about the metropolis, it's long been one of the best places in town. The LTB has some branches, which we've listed in the appropriate areas. Neither head office nor the branches offer a telephone enquiry service – there are, however, a series of premium-rate recorded services, including seasonal information and events. For a list of these, ring (020) 7971 0026. / Times: Easter-Oct 8am-7pm; otherwise Mon-Sat 8am-6pm, Sun 8.30am-4pm; www.londontown.com; Tube: Victoria.

Britain Visitor Centre W1

1 Regent St   2–2C

As its name suggests, this office not far from Piccadilly Circus is a good source of information about Britain generally, as well as about London. / Times: Mon-Fri 9am-6.30pm, Sat & Sun 10am-4pm; Tube: Piccadilly Circus.

Public Transport Enquiries SW1

Victoria Station   (020) 7222 1234   2–4B

This 24-hour telephone service is an invaluable source of help for any queries about services run by Transport for London (which runs the Underground, London Buses, the Docklands Light Railway, River Services and Victoria Coach Station).

The Travel Information Office on the concourse of Victoria Station (opposite platform 8) is an excellent source of maps and brochures to enable you to use London's public transport efficiently.

There are also TICs at: Heathrow Terminals 1, 2 and 4; and at the Terminals 1, 2, and 3 Underground stations (Mon-Sat); West Croydon, Euston; Hammersmith (Mon-Sat); Piccadilly Circus; St James's Park (Mon-Fri); Liverpool Street; Oxford Circus (closed Sun); Kings Cross; Paddington (Mon-Sun).

A series of free leaflets entitled Simply London – with information on various subjects from discovering East London to shopping for food – is available from most Underground stations or from their website. / Times: office open 8.15am (Sun 8.45am)-7.30pm; www.transportforlondon.gov.uk; Tube: Victoria.

Londonwide information

Capital helplines
(020) 7484 4000
Capital Radio's all-year information line, Contact Capital, will try to answer your questions – however practical, or offbeat. At various times of year, Capital also offers special helplines (numbers vary) such as revision lines (before GCSEs) and the Christmas line – a useful source of information over the period when London closes up and dies from Christmas Eve to Boxing Day. One of the most popular lines is the Flatshare service (tel (020) 7484 8000). It is free to advertise a vacant room and lists are published in The Guardian on Thu or are available free of charge, from 4pm Fri, from Capital Radio at 30 Leicester Square WC2. Listen in to 95.8 FM for details of the occasional services. / Times: helpline: Mon-Fri 9am-9pm; www.capitalfm.com;

Newspapers

TNT
It may not be quite as comprehensive as Time Out *(which is free only on consultation in public libraries), but* TNT *– the weekly magazine for expat Aussies and Kiwis – is obtainable without any charge and has quite good theatre, cinema and other event listings. It also includes details of the many free slide shows organised by the main trekking and adventure companies to publicise their holidays. There are also articles of general budget interest, too. Pick a copy up from the publication's spiritual home – outside Earl's Court tube – or from street dispensers throughout central London, including major rail and tube stations.*

Metro
Metro is a daily free newspaper which can be picked up at Underground stations each weekday morning – look for the blue metal dump bins. You'll need to be quick, as they're usually all gone by 9am. In addition to general news, it has listings of events happening that day, including free or inexpensive sources of entertainment. / www.metro.co.uk.

Ms London, Girl About Town, Nine to Five, Midweek, London Monthly
A range of magazines aimed at differing sections of London's inhabitants (South Africans, Canadians, South Americans...) is available from dump bins outside principal tube and rail stations. As well as articles, listings and reviews, they often include discount vouchers for services and even the occasional offer for a free haircut.

Other information

Alternative Arts
(020) 7375 0441
This organisation provides a platform for various performing artists, and strives to make the arts easily accessible for the general public. For this reason, events (which range from outdoor opera performances to African dance and drama) are all free and happen in public places – Victoria Embankment Gardens WC2 and Berkeley Square W1, for example. For details of what's on during the year send an SAE to Alternative Arts, 47a Brushfield Street, London E1 6AA – the annual calendar is available from Oct of the previous year.

Books
This book is a general guide, designed as an introduction to the many free delights which London has to offer. There are of course many special interests which you can pursue in London without cost, upon which there is much more information available than we are able to set out here. The following are some of the most handy books currently in print – you can also borrow them from a library – to give you more information. The best, most comprehensive, general guide is probably the Eyewitness Travel Guide, *with listings, pictures and descriptions of galleries, museums, walks and architecture. Other guides of note include those published by Fodor's, Rough Guides and Lonely Planet.* Museums and Galleries of London *(Abigail Willis, 2001) provides an intelligent overview of its subject, without going into so much detail as to put off the general reader.* London Markets *(Phil Harris, 2001) tells you everything you might want to know about the capital's colourful street life. The* Time Out Book of London Walks *(2001) provides an interesting collection of intellectual, cultural and historical peregrinations.*

City of London Churches
The churches of the City (many by Wren) are among London's greatest architectural treasures. A leaflet, available from the City of London Information Centre (see City section), actually lists all buildings of historical and architectural interest within the Square Mile. Opening times, maps, the nearest tube stations and suggested walking routes are included, as well as a brief history of the City and sketches of the buildings described.

Londonwide information

Disabled access

There are several services which are very helpful for disabled people who are exploring London.

General queries relating in any way to travel for the disabled and elderly (and including information about hire of vehicles) can be addressed to Tripscope (Alexandra House, Albany Road, Brentford, Middlesex TW8 0NE; tel: (020) 8580 7021). Transport for London offers a free guide to public transport, available from TfL Access & Mobility (tel: (020) 7941 4600; e-mail: access&mobility@tfl.gov.uk).

To check out the details of the access arrangements for any place of entertainment or tourist attraction in London you can call Artsline (54 Chalton Street, London NW1 1HS; (020) 7388 2227). Artsline also publishes a range of access guides, including some to tourist attractions (nominal charge). Also worth consulting is www.theatre-access.co.uk, which holds details on disabled access to the capital's theatres. For those interested in finding physical activities, The British Sports Association for the Disabled also has a useful website – www.disabilitysports.org.uk, where one can find information on trampolining and swimming groups, amongst others.

Galleries

London remains one of the great centres of the international market in pictures and objets d'art. Much of the business is conducted through galleries to which the public has free access.

We can't lead you to the changing artistic attractions of the capital, as many of the most interesting commercial shows last for only a month or so. However, help is at hand in the form of an excellent monthly publication – Galleries – of which you can obtain a copy, gratis, from almost any commercial art gallery. Its handy format contains a wealth of information, helpfully organised into areas (with maps) and indexed in every way you could possibly want (including by artist and type of work). It also contains short but interesting articles on many of the forthcoming attractions. Many other publications, such as Time Out, also provide comprehensive listings.

You could easily spend a week just exploring London's commercial galleries. As a starting point, the greatest concentrations are found around Cork Street, Bruton Street and Old Bond Street W1, and in St James's SW1. There are also clusters of galleries around the junction of Portobello Road and Westbourne Grove W11 and in Walton Street SW3. Those in search of more 'alternative' displays should head north or east, to Camden, Islington and Hoxton – the area around Old Street and Clerkenwell Road EC1 is especially fertile.

The great auction houses are a fascinating part of the art world – details are given in the Central section.

London Lesbian & Gay Switchboard

(020) 7837 7324

This voluntary organisation offers a 24-hour information, support and advice helpline to lesbians and gay men. (Other sources of information include the free magazines and newspapers available in most gay bars.) / www.llgs.org.uk.

Museums

The 24 Hour Museum is a charitable organisation funded by the Department of Culture, Media & Sport – it aims to promote British museums and the facilities they offer. The website (www.24hourmuseum.org.uk) provides information on current exhibitions and an online magazine, and links to museums' own websites (where applicable). Not all of the museums listed are free. Events taking place in Museums and Galleries Month (usually in May each year) are listed on this site.

Parks

The myriad parks and open spaces of London are managed by various organisations. For detailed information not listed under individual park entries (see the index on page 163 for the list of entries).

Information about the Royal Parks is to be found at www.royalparks.co.uk. The site which covers comprehensive historical detail and forthcoming events in the 8,000 acres of London parkland still owned by the Crown.

The Corporation of London (www.cityoflondon.gov.uk) manages over 10,000 acres of green space, woodland and parks (150 sites in the Square Mile alone, as well as Queen's Park, Epping Forest and Hampstead Heath). Call (020) 8472 3584 for a leaflet on the City.

Walks

One of the very best – and completely free – ways to get to know London is to walk. The bus routes mentioned in the introduction are an excellent way of connecting areas, and 'seeing the sights', but there is no match for being able to nip down intriguing alleys, investigate churches, visit urban parks, wander along canals, pop into pubs or just meander at will. Some of the books we have recommended offer interesting walks with various themes, and we have suggested walks at the front of each geographical section in this book. In addition, the Green Chain Walk (see South) links many of south London's parks and open spaces.

Londonwide information

Another excellent source of information and walk routes is the London Walking Forum (www.londonwalking.com), a partnership of organisations in and around London that have an interest in or responsibility for walking. Amongst other projects and footpath improvements made since the forum was established in 1990, a 150 mile (240 km) circular walk through the best of outer London's countryside has been created. It is broken into 24 manageable sections, all conveniently connected to public transport. Environmental improvements, better signing and guided walks are other projects of the organisation.

The Internet

There are lots of internet cafés around London, offering free browsing with your cup of coffee (as well as the dedicated internet shops, such as Easy Everything, which charge an hourly, but fairly small, rate for their services). However, the savvy traveller should know that there are many opportunities for completely free web browsing in the capital – you just need to know where to look. Some libraries and museums offer free internet access. In some cases this is simply for browsing, but others will have no objection if you reply to all your e-mails. The Oxford Circus branch of Topshop has computers for free use, as do many bars (the Vibe Bar in Brick Lane, E1, for example), and Debenhams store in Oxford Street, offers 30 minutes' free browsing with every purchase.

We have listed websites with entries in this guide where possible. Some useful general websites for visitors include: www.thisislondon.co.uk (from the owners of the Evening Standard and Metro newspapers); www.londontown.com (from the London Tourist Board); www.streetmap.co.uk (maps to help you find your way around) and www.london-daily.co.uk (London newspaper).

Many of the attractions and buildings listed here are cared for by one of two national heritage bodies, English Heritage (www.english-heritage.org.uk) and The National Trust (www.nationaltrust.org.uk). Their websites contain further information on the sites and attractions for which they are responsible.

Other activities

If, as we assume, you already have a Travelcard, you can explore London from the best possible vantage point – the upper platform of a double-decker bus – at no cost. This form of tour has the virtue that you can hop on and hop off to your heart's content. If you find there are so many things to do you don't have time to finish your planned circuit, it hardly matters.

With one of Transport for London's free bus guides, you can plan your own tour, but there are two routes which are particularly suitable for a general orientation.

The number 11 takes you on a great East-West tour of London, and includes many of the major sights. Start your trip at a stop in Chelsea's fashionable King's Road and ride through Victoria to Westminster Abbey. This would be a good place to break the journey and to walk a short way – through Parliament Square, and down Whitehall to look at 10 Downing Street and the Cenotaph. Get back on the bus at Trafalgar Square – having admired Nelson's Column and, if time permits, visited the National Gallery. Travel down the Strand and Fleet Street, and end at St Paul's Cathedral.

The number 15 (pick it up at Paddington, Edgware Road, Oxford Street or Regent Street) shares the Trafalgar Square to St Paul's section with the number 11 (so you can change at any point between the two). However, the 15 continues on into the City enabling you to see the Monument, Tower Bridge and the Tower of London. Travel on this route on a Sunday morning and you might press on to Aldgate, for Petticoat Lane market.

Courts
If you have half a day to kill, you might find it interesting, and perhaps amusing, to spend it in court. There are three types of court which will be within easy reach of most parts of London – Magistrates, Crown and County Courts.

All human life passes through London's magistrates courts, where the highest and the lowest appear to explain why they have (or have not) committed minor criminal offences, from drunkenness to speeding. Sometimes it will be pretty humdrum stuff (if not without human interest), but if you hit lucky, you may experience a real trial, probably not lasting more than a day, where the question "did he (or she) do it?" is of more than academic interest, especially to the person in the dock.

In the Crown courts, the more serious crimes – all the way up to murder – are tried by a bewigged judge and a jury. The disadvantage for the casual visitor is that most trials go on for several days, so inevitably you will see only a fraction of the proceedings. By far the most interesting theatre is to be found when a witness (especially the defendant) is being cross-examined by the opposing side's counsel. The Old Bailey (see The City) is London's senior Crown court.

County Courts resolve civil disputes (such as claims for damages, perhaps arising from a motor accident, or unpaid debts). Again, cross-examination is generally by far the most gripping part of a trial. The most important civil trials take place at the Royal Courts of Justice (see The City).

Londonwide information

For the address of your local court, consult the telephone directory. Courts generally sit between 10am and 4.30pm. Children under 16 are not usually admitted into the public galleries. / www.courtservice.gov.uk.

Fire Stations
It may be possible to organise a visit to your local fire brigade. Write to the Commander at your nearest station.

London Cyclist
Try your local library for the bi-monthly magazine of the very active London Cycling Campaign (tel (020) 7928 7220, Mon-Fri 2pm-5pm). Every issue has details of social, weekend rides, and in summer, and during the Festival of Cycling (second week in June), evening and early morning rides. All rides are guided and free (although some may involve train journeys).

Volunteers at bi-monthly 'stuffing' evenings (putting copies of London Cyclist into envelopes reading for posting) are rewarded with free vegetarian food and the chance to swap details of potholes and near-misses with a range of like-minded people. During Bike Week there are several cyclists' breakfasts – more free grub if you can get up early enough to pedal off and join in! / www.lcc.org.uk.

London Wildlife Trust SE1
Halling House, 47-51 Great Suffolk St   (020) 7261 0447
The Trust's aim is to sustain and enhance London's wildlife habitats, and to this end it manages 57 nature reserves – a free map of locations is available. Each year, more than 600 free indoor and outdoor events, classes and volunteer opportunities are organised – from bat walks to wild flower talks. Call the number given to obtain information packs and factsheets, as well as details and locations of volunteer contacts throughout London. / www.wildlifetrust.org.uk.

Royal Society of Art WC2
8 John Adam St   (020) 7930 5115   2–2C
The Royal Society for the Encouragement of Arts, Manufactures and Commerce (to give it its full name) is located just off the Strand, in a house that was designed especially for the Society by Robert Adam in the 1770s. A programme of around 40 lectures a year takes place between October and May. Lectures are primarily aimed at members, but non-members are welcome to attend if they apply in advance for a ticket. The range of subjects is wide, and has recently included, 'Movement in the Millennium' and 'Should we end Immigration Controls?'. There is also a free Christmas lecture each year for children. / www.rsa.org.uk; Tube: Embankment, Charing Cross.

Shane English School W1
59 South Molton St   (020) 7499 8533   2–2B
*Learn (or improve) your English for free on a four-week course
in Central London. Every four weeks a new intake of teachers
on a month-long programme leading to a recognised
qualification of teaching English as a foreign language (TEFL)
need a class to practise on. Around 15 places are available at
elementary and intermediate levels. Would-be students must
commit themselves for the full duration and pay a £20 deposit
which they receive back on completion of the course.*
/ Times: Mon-Fri 2pm-4.30pm; www.shane-english.co.uk; Tube: Bond Street.

Volunteering

One unusual way to enjoy London is to get involved in
one of the many volunteer groups. Long-term
commitments are often required for work in charity
shops, for example, but we have listed some of the
organisations who may welcome just a day or two's hard
work from a helper. Free tea and coffee or even lunch are
often provided. The London Wildlife Trust and London
Cyclist (both listed above, page 18) also have volunteer
requirements.

BTCV
(People Working for Better Environment) N1
80 York Way   (020) 7278 4294   4–3C
*Get some fresh air, and brush up your 'green' skills with BTCV
– the largest organisation in the United Kingdom promoting
practical conservation work by volunteers. Its projects range
from building footbridges to managing woodland, and
volunteers are always welcome. Training is always provided –
no experience is necessary. The website gives details of a wide
range of courses, access to most of which is free.* / Times: Mon-Fri
9am-5pm; www.btcv.org.uk; Tube: King's Cross.

Surrey Docks Farm BS3
The Federation of City Farms, The Green House,
Hereford St, Bedminster, Bristol   (0117) 923 1800
*This organisation holds details of all the city farms and
community gardens in Britain – most of which will almost
certainly have ongoing requirements for volunteers. Surrey
Docks Farm and Spitalfields City Farm are among those
always looking for extra help. (See index for a list of London
city farms.)*

Gunnersbury Triangle Nature Reserve W4
Bollo Ln   (020) 8747 3881   1–3A
*This intriguing nature reserve makes use of volunteers in
practical management and administrative positions. Interested
parties can call or simply turn up. (See entry, page 76.)*
/ Times: Tue, Sun; Tube: Chiswick Park.

Londonwide information

Heath Hands
(Volunteers for Hampstead Heath) NW3
Greenmoor, Vale of Health   (020) 7794 6772
Heath Hands is a volunteer group that helps the Corporation of London make Hampstead Heath even greener. Activities include garden maintenance, tree work and bird box construction. The organisation is happy to welcome helpers who are only able to assist for a day or two – you must call in advance to make sure there are enough tools on the day you wish to help out. Volunteers must be at least 16 years old. / www.heath-hands.org.uk.

The Age Reminiscence Centre SE3
11 Blackheath Village   (020) 8318 9105   1–4D
For full details of the Age Reminiscence Centre see page 100. If you like the idea of working for older folk, you might like to consider acting as a volunteer. / Times: Mon-Sat 10am-5.30pm; www.ageexchange.org.uk; BR: Blackheath.

The Thames 21 Project
(020) 7248 2916
Set up in 1994, the Project's aim is to improve and enhance the environment of London's rivers, and it removes hundreds of tons of litter annually. If you're interested in helping out – on a regular or 'one-off' basis – visit the website or call the number given. / www.thames21.org.uk.

Thrive E2
corner of Pearson St & Appleby St   (020) 7739 2965
Founded in 1978, this national charity uses 'therapeutic horticulture' to improve the lives of disabled, disadvantaged and older people. Two of their garden projects are in London, in Bethnal Green and Battersea. Volunteers are always required to work in the gardens – no gardening experience is necessary. / Times: Mon-Fri 9.30am-5pm; www.thrive.org.uk; Tube: Liverpool Street, Old Street.

Waterway Recovery Group
Rickmansworth   (01923) 711114
A volunteer organisation helping to restore derelict canals. Wish to be kept abreast of their 'dirty weekend' possibilities (as they call them)? – register on the website for a newsletter. / www.wrg.org.uk

Events

Regular events

Ceremony of the Keys EC3
Tower of London   (020) 7709 0765
In accordance with seven centuries of tradition, the Tower of London (home, of course, to the Crown Jewels) is secured for the night with a brief ceremony. Anyone can apply for a ticket to attend, but you need to do so in writing enclosing an SAE (Ceremony of the Keys, The Operations Department, HM Tower of London, London EC3N 4AB) stating the names and addresses of those in your group and the date you would like to attend, giving at least two months' notice. / Times: nightly at 9.30pm; www.tower-of-london.com/traditions; Tube: Tower Hill.

Changing the Guard (Buckingham Palace) SW1
(0891) 505452 recorded information
The changing of the sentries at Buckingham Palace is famous around the world. The new guard leaves Wellington Barracks three minutes before the change, and, preceded by a band, marches down Birdcage Walk to the palace. The ceremony lasts 40 minutes, and takes place inside the railings of the palace itself. The event is subject to cancellation in very bad weather or during state visits. In conjunction with this event, the St James's Palace detachment of the Queen's Guard marches to Buckingham Palace at 11.15am and back to St James's Palace at 12.10pm. / Times: Apr-Oct, daily at 11.30am; Nov-Mar, every other day; www.londontown.com/guards.phtml; Tube: Green Park.

Changing the Guard (Horse Guards) SW1
Horse Guards Parade
(0891) 505452 recorded information
In a daily burst of pageantry, a mounted guard leaves Hyde Park Barracks at 10.28am (Sun 9.28am) and proceeds, via Hyde Park Corner and Constitution Hill, to arrive at Horse Guards Parade at 11am (Sun 10am), where the guard is changed. The splendidly attired mounted guardsmen making their way through Hyde Park offers what is probably London's most romantic sight. / Times: daily at 11am, Sun 10am; www.londontown.com/guards.phtml; Tube: Hyde Park Corner, St James's Park.

Gun Salutes
One of the most striking sights in London is the gun salutes which hail royal and state events. These take place in Green, St James's, or Hyde Park (12 noon) and at the Tower of London (1pm) on the following dates (or, if a Sunday, the next day): 6 February (Accession Day); 21 April (the Queen's birthday); 2 June (Coronation Day); 10 June (the Duke of Edinburgh's birthday); and 4 August (the Queen Mother's birthday). Salutes also mark state visits (usually in May and October), Trooping the Colour (June) and the State Opening of Parliament (October or November). Details of these and other events in the Royal Parks are given in the Summer Entertainment Programme available with an A5 SAE from the Old Police House, Hyde Park, London W2 2UH (tel (020) 7298 2000). / www.royalparks.co.uk; Tube: Hyde Park Corner, Tower Hill.

Annual timetable

Barely a month goes by in London without some great event happening which can provide a good focus for a day out, especially with children in tow. The major events which happen on an annual basis are as follows.

January

London Parade
(020) 8566 8586
The New Year starts with a bang as an American-style family event takes place on the first day of the year. Hundreds of thousands of people turn out to see the big parade, with 6,000 majorettes (flown in from the States), clowns, floats and dance displays. It starts from Parliament Square at noon and the final band reaches Berkeley Square in Mayfair around 3pm. The procession (for which Whitehall or Piccadilly offer the best vantage points) consists of marching bands, floats and horse-drawn carriages, in which ride the Archbishop and Lord Mayor of Westminster and mayors of all the London boroughs (but not, of course, the fiercely independent City).
/ www.londonparade.co.uk; Tube: Westminster, St James's Park, Green Park.

Mime Festival*
(020) 7637 5661
Many different theatrical and visual art shows and exhibitions take place at several venues throughout the week. Most of the events require the purchase of a ticket, but some are free. The festival features performers from the UK, Spain, Russia, Poland, France and Belgium and covers exhibitions and performances from circus performance to overhead projections to puppets.
/ www.mimefest.co.uk.

Chinese New Year
In late January or early February, Chinatown celebrates the Chinese New Year with noisy, colourful parades (including the famous papier mâché dragons), which last most of the day (11am-6.30pm). The whole area (around Gerrard Street W1) is brightly decorated for the event. / Tube: Leicester Square.

Events

Pancake Day Races

Covent Garden WC2/Spitalfields Market E1
(020) 7375 0441 (Alternative Arts)
*Shrove Tuesday ('Pancake Day') sees traditional races
between pancake-tossing relay-teams at Covent Garden
(check newspapers for times) and Spitalfields (12.30pm).*
/ Tube: Covent Garden, Leicester Square, Liverpool Street.

March

Head of the River Race

(01932) 220401
*The Oxford and Cambridge Boat Race may be more famous,
but, for the casual observer, the Head of the River race, rowed
on a Saturday in March from Mortlake to Putney, is probably
more interesting to watch. The sheer number of crews (usually
over 400) means that the colourful procession of eight-oared
boats (which are set off 10 seconds apart) takes well over an
hour. Being a timed race, it does have the disadvantage that
no one knows who has won until it's all over. Best vantage
points are as for the Boat Race (below), but those in the know
go to Chiswick Bridge to watch the pre-race marshalling of
hundreds of boats in a confined stretch of the river. Start times
vary according to the tides.* / www.horr.co.uk; Tube: Putney Bridge.

Oxford & Cambridge Boat Race

*It may be an arcane and thoroughly English way of spending
an afternoon, but the world's most famous boat race, between
Oxford and Cambridge University Boat Clubs, continues to
exercise an extraordinary grip on the popular imagination.
Tens of thousands of people turn out every year to snatch a
passing glimpse of an 18-minute race (first rowed on the
Thames in 1849) which, from a practical point of view, is much
better watched on television. The best vantage points for the
four-mile race from Putney to Mortlake are generally held to be
at the half-way point (Hammersmith) or at the finish – but you
don't get much of a view anywhere and the real point is not
really the race but the atmosphere. Take a picnic and – if
you want to know who's won – a radio.* / www.theboatrace.org;
Tube: Hammersmith, Putney Bridge.

April

Flora London Marathon
(020) 7620 4117
The London Marathon, first run in 1981, has grown into a huge event which attracts more than 30,000 runners and over half a million spectators annually. Its sheer scale and spectacle makes it a good family day out. Over half of the runners are taking part for charity (and collectively raise over £10 million). Many run in costume, and you may see some famous faces. The course of just over 26 miles begins (around 9am) on Blackheath and ends (having taken a circuitous route) outside Buckingham Palace. The leading runners take a little over two hours to complete the course, but the stragglers ensure it's practically an all-day event. / www.london-marathon.co.uk.

Kite Festival SE3
Blackheath
Easter Sunday and Monday see London's leading annual kite festival – a great spectacle whether you're interested in kite-flying or not. (Devotees might like to note there are also two smaller events in the summer – here and in Hackney Marshes.) / BR: Blackheath.

May

Canalway Cavalcade W9
Pool of Little Venice, Paddington   (0192) 371 1114
Watercrafts of all types take part in the colourful boat rally organised by the Inland Waterways Association. In conjunction, this lively, family event boasts live music, Morris dancing, a teddy bear picnic, boat trips and waterway-related trade and craft stalls. An evening highlight is the illuminated boat procession which takes place on the Sunday. / Times: May Day bank hol weekend, 10am-6pm & Sun eve; www.waterways.org.uk; Tube: Warwick Avenue.

Coin Street Festival SE1
Gabriel's Wharf; Bernie Spain Gardens; Oxo Tower Wharf
(020) 7928 0960, recorded info (020) 7401 2255
A popular and growing annual event that runs from mid-June to September, and which celebrates the many cultures and interests of the people who live, work in, or visit the capital. Highlights are live music and street performances – from French street theatre to African storytelling – and there are many activities for children, including workshops and competitions. Almost every weekend there is a day of events, all of which are free, usually around a particular theme – call for a leaflet. / www.coinstreetfestival.org; Tube: Waterloo, Blackfriars, Southwark.

Events

Covent Garden Festival* WC2
67 Long Acre   (020) 7379 0870
During the festival, a stage is put up at the west end of Covent Garden Piazza and a range of opera and musical works are performed. Some of the events are free; call for a festival brochure, or visit the website to see the timetable of events.
/ www.cgf.co.uk; Tube: Covent Garden, Leicester Square.

Museums & Galleries Month*
During May and early June, around 850 museums in the capital and across the country – including many of the free institutions listed in this book – put on special events. (This event was previously Museums Week.) Full details appear in the Radio Times and on the website.
/ www.museumsweek.org.uk.

May Fayre & Puppet Festival WC2
St Paul's Church & Gardens, Bedford St
(020) 7375 0441 (Alternative Arts)
This all-day event, which takes place on the nearest Sunday to 9 May, celebrates the art of puppetry, with Punch and Judy performers from all over the country. There's a parade at 10.30am and a service in St Paul's Church, from 11.30am.
/ Times: 10.30am-5.30pm; Tube: Covent Garden, Leicester Square.

June

City of London Festival* EC2
City Festival Box Office, St Paul's Churchyard, London
EC4M 8BU   (020) 7377 1942
In late June/early July, the City enjoys an explosion of music. If you're looking for free events, seek out the world music series which takes place on weekday lunchtimes at venues throughout the Square Mile. The festival's Opening Service is effectively a sung eucharist followed by a free choral concert in the magnificent setting of St Paul's. There is almost invariably a charge for the evening events. / www.colf.org.

Devizes to Westminster International Canoe Race
Often referred to as the 'Canoeist's Everest', this claims to be the world's toughest canoe race, lasting for three days and 125 miles. It has been raced every Easter since 1948, along the Kennet and Avon Canal to Reading, where it enters the Thames. You can watch the end of the race, at Westminster Bridge (usually around 9am on Mon morning) from the relative comfort of the Embankment. / www.dw-perspective.org.uk.

Henley Royal Regatta*
(01491) 572153
tourist info (01491) 578034
Henley, established in 1839, is the world's oldest major rowing regatta. It takes place in late June/early July (the final Sunday is always the 27th Sunday of the year). Even if you've never been in a rowing boat in your life, and even if you don't know anyone who is a member of one of the enclosures, it's still one of the most enjoyable events of the 'Season' and manages, to an extraordinary extent, to maintain something of the atmosphere of an Edwardian garden party. Take a picnic, arrive early, and find a good viewpoint along the towpath – all but the last third of a mile or so of the course is open to the public, and at many points you can hear the commentary. The event lasts from Wednesday to Sunday – it's much less crowded on the weekdays. / www.hrr.co.uk; BR: Henley on Thames.

Mardi Gras*
London's major lesbian and gay festival takes place in late June/early July. The event (for which there is a charge) usually includes an impressive line-up of world-renowned musical artists, and follows a colourful street march and float parade (actually organised by Pride, who used to run the whole event) which is free for all to watch. The parade usually starts from Hyde Park Corner at noon; check newspapers or the website for the precise route. / www.londonmardigras.com.

Spitalfields Summer Festival* E1
Christ Church, Commercial St   Hotline (020) 7377 1362
Hawksmoor's imposing Christ Church is the setting for two annual classical music festivals – the other one is held just before Christmas. There is a varied programme of lunchtime and evening concerts of music from c15 to contemporary. There are also complementary exhibitions and a fringe festival, including arts events, comedy and circus performances. Call or check the website for further details. / Times: church, Mon-Fri 12pm-2.30pm & Sun between services; festival, details from hotline; www.spitalfieldsfestival.org.uk; Tube: Shoreditch, Liverpool Street, Aldgate East.

Stoke Newington Festival* N16
Box Office, c/o Stoke Newington Library Foyer,
Stoke Newington Church St   (020) 8356 6411
This annual independent arts festival stretches across four weekends in June and showcases Hackney-based artists, performers and musicians. The festival kicks off with a large outdoor street festival, usually on the second Sunday of the month. Many events, including poetry readings, walks and listening to the dawn chorus, are free. Visual arts events, including installations and photographic exhibitions, take place in unusual settings including Abney Park Cemetery (see also). / www.stokenewingtonfestival.co.uk; BR: Stoke Newington or 73 bus.

Trooping the Colour*
(020) 7930 4466
A Saturday in early June sees the celebration of the Queen's Official Birthday, when she inspects an elaborate military display at Horse Guards Parade SW1. At 1pm, after her return to Buckingham Palace, there is an RAF flypast down the Mall.

There is a charge to attend the event itself (although, of course, you can watch the procession down the Mall), but tickets for the first rehearsal, The Major General's Review are free, (two or three Saturdays before), and (as for the main event) are allocated by ballot. Apply in January or February, with an SAE, to Brigade Major (Trooping the Colour), Headquarters, Household Division, Horse Guards, Whitehall London SW1A 2AX. Check newspapers or www.londontown.com for times and dates. / Tube: St James's Park.

Vauxhall Festival
(020) 7793 0263 (Vauxhall St Peter's Heritage Centre)
Local organisations and individuals take the stage at Vauxhall St Peter's Heritage Centre for a variety of arts and community events, highlighting the local contemporary arts scene. The last day is an all-day outdoor music festival.

Flower Festival WC2
The Piazza   recorded info (09064) 701777
Taking place annually in the last week of June in this former fruit and veg market, the Festival (begun in 1997) presents innovative and contemporary flower displays and garden installations combined with theatrical productions and promotions. It focuses on new designs, products and services and is aimed particularly at the urban gardener. The festival has its own catwalk show called Fashion Flowers, in which floral accessories and even complete outfits are made solely of flowers. The main attraction is the performance garden, a large-scale installation in front of St Paul's Church, offering a platform for street theatre, opera, music and dance. There are also displays and promotions in the Seven Dials area, a short stroll north of Covent Garden piazza. / www.cgff.co.uk; Tube: Covent Garden, Leicester Square.

July

Croydon Summer Festival*, Surrey
(020) 8253 1009
Previously known as the Croydon Jazz Week (which was well-known for its traditional jazz), the arts festival now encompasses a wide range of live music, including street performance, Caribbean and Latin, as well as jazz. A highlight is the Croydon Mela, London's second largest Asian music festival. Most of the free events take place at lunchtime. A full brochure of events is available approximately two months prior to the festival, which lasts for two weeks in July.
/ www.croydon.gov.uk.

Dogget's Coat & Badge Race
The oldest event in British sport, this sculling race takes place from Chelsea to London Bridge (or the Coat and Badge pub, to be precise). It was in 1751 that Thomas Dogget, an Irish actor and comedian, funded the first race, to commemorate the accession of George I. Originally restricted to 'professional watermen' only, the rules have been relaxed to permit amateurs in recent years.

Ealing Countryside Weekend
Berkeley Fields, opposite Ballot Box pub, Horsenden Ln North, Greenford   020 8758 5916
One of the biggest waterside events in London. Attractions include dancing, international food stalls, farm activities, a craft village and environmental displays. Full details are available from June. / Times: Sat 12pm-10pm, Sun 11am-8pm; www.ealing.gov.uk; Tube: Greenford, Perivale.

Ealing Summer Festival*
(020) 8758 5743
Ealing's annual Summer Festival is a month-long series of events, including the Ealing Blues 'n' Groove Party and the International Food Fair. In the lead-up to the actual festival in Walpole Park, a roadshow takes place in several of the borough's other parks. Entertainment, some of which is free (especially during the day), includes shows and activities for children, arena displays, comedy, theatrical performances and sports events. The festival is immediately followed by the Ealing Jazz Festival (see also). / www.ealing.gov.uk/summer; Tube: Ealing Broadway.

Hillingdon Borough Carnival
Hayes, Middx   (01895) 250648 (Recreational Services)
Every year the second weekend in July sees the streets of Hayes erupt with floats and crowds. Up to 20 floats, followed by marching bands, lead the way from Pump Lane at 12.30pm, to Barra Hall Park. Here there is a funfair, Punch and Judy shows, clowns, stalls, pony rides, live music and stilt-walking. / www.hillingdon.gov.uk; BR: Hayes and Harlington.

Events

Swan Upping
(020) 7236 1863

All the swans on the Thames between London Bridge and Henley belong to the Queen or one of two of the City livery companies: the Dyers and the Vintners. This cosy three-way arrangement has been in place since 1510. Each year, it is necessary to mark the cygnets to show to whom they belong (which depends on who owns their parents). This task is carried out every July, by a procession of six 'Thames Skiffs' (rowed by colourfully-uniformed oarsmen), which takes a week to progress from Sunbury to Sonning. When swans are spotted, the traditional cry of "All-up" is raised, and they are coralled by three skiffs, one staffed by each of the potential owners, in preparation for identification and marking. The swans, it seems, do not always come quietly. If you want to know when and where you can witness this extraordinary ritual, call the Vintners on the number given. Traditionally, swans were marked by nicking their beaks, but they are now ringed instead – in deference to tradition, the practice is, of course, known as 'nicking'.

Greenwich & Docklands International Festival*
(020) 8305 1818

This multi-arts extravaganza now spans both banks of the Thames (and much of east London). Many of the attractions are free and include opening and closing night pyrotechnics, open-air music and dance performances. For details, you can visit the website or ring the festival hotline. / www.festival.org; Tube: Greenwich, Woolwich (DLR).

August

Croydon Forestry Country Show
Selsdon Wood, Old Farleigh Rd   (020) 8253 1009

A family day out in the countryside. Features include falconry displays, classic cars, pony rides, ancient (but working) farm machinery and rare breeds of farm animals. / www.croydon.gov.uk; BR: East Croydon & then 64 bus to Selsdon & then free shuttle to show ground.

Ealing Jazz Festival
(020) 8758 5743

After 16 years in existence, the 'friendly festival' – so-called because of its family atmosphere – claims to be the largest free jazz festival in Britain. Lunchtime and evening concerts are led by musicians, playing fusion, Latin and modern jazz on a stage in Walpole Park. The festival takes place during the first week of August, on the back end of the Ealing Summer Festival (see also). / www.ealing.gov.uk/jazz; Tube: Ealing Broadway.

Notting Hill Carnival

The August bank holiday sees the largest street party in Europe – over a million people attending a musical celebration of Afro-Caribbean culture. The carnival is centred around the northern parts of the Portobello Road. Sunday sees the Children's Carnival Day, while the main procession of floats takes place on Monday. There is music for all tastes, including reggae, jazz, hip-hop and house. The whole event is certainly impressive in its sheer scale and vitality, but this may make it seem rather daunting to some people. All the common-sense rules of attending such a large and crowded occasion apply – don't drive there, keep hold of children, carry as little money as possible, and don't hang around once the daytime festivities are over. Leave your English reserve at home and the music and atmosphere might well transport you to the Caribbean!
/ www.nottinghillcarnival.net.uk; Tube: Notting Hill Gate, Ladbroke Grove.

September

Angel Canal Festival N1

City Road Basin, Regent's Canal, off Wharf Rd
(020) 7267 9100
This annual community festival celebrates the Regent's Canal in Islington, and is based around City Road Lock and Basin. Usually held on the first Sunday in September, the festival features a variety of stalls, a fun-fair, music, boat trips and a Regatta. / Times: 11.30am-5.30pm; Tube: Angel.

Great River Race

c/o Stuart Wolff (020) 8398 9057
This ever more popular event has all the ingredients of a Great British Success Story. For a start, the idea behind it is completely – inspiringly – batty. Take more than 250 oared boats (rule: no racing-boats allowed), devise a handicapping system (which allows some boats to start 100 minutes before others) and set them off (down a tidal river) on a 22-mile journey from Ham House in Richmond to Island Gardens on the Isle of Dogs. The event attracts every type of boat (from Chinese dragon boats to Hawaiian war canoes) and rowers and paddlers of all ages and of every degree of seriousness from all over the world. It's a wonderful spectacle, and one which can be viewed from any London bank of the Thames, though the greatest excitement is of course at the start, at Richmond, (12.30pm) and the finish: best viewing by the Cutty Sark, in Greenwich (4.15pm-4.30pm). / www.greatriverrace.co.uk; Tube: choice of 12 riverside stations between Richmond and Island Gardens (DLR).

Events

Heritage Open Days

(020) 7930 0914

The Civic Trust co-ordinates an annual exercise which allows the public to see, for free, buildings of historic or architectural interest that are usually closed to general enquirers. The celebration takes place in the second weekend of September and highlights various properties, from windmills to music halls, throughout England. For details of the buildings that will be open, write to Heritage Open Day, Civic Trust, 17 Carlton House Terrace, London SW1Y 5AW, enclosing six second-class stamps or check the website, on which the buildings are listed by area. / www.civictrust.org.uk.

London Festival of Literature* EC1

245 St John St   (020) 7837 2555

The first annual festival, held in 2000, saw a programme of over 100 events occurring all over London, from author readings and discussions to children's days. Many events took place at Shakespeare's Globe on the South Bank; some, but by no means all, of the events were free. Call or visit the website for the dates of the next festival. / www.theword.org.uk.

London Open House

Hotline (60p/min) 0900 1600 061

Heritage Open Day (see above) is a national event. The London equivalent takes place a week later. On these dates the public can gain free admittance to all types of buildings, from cinemas and colleges to theatres, even perhaps a former mortuary, which are not normally accessible. There are over 500 buildings open to the public for free. There are also walks, exhibitions and lectures. The idea is to celebrate London's wealth of architecture, to promote public awareness of architecture and the built environment and to encourage civic pride. In addition, there are building tours and activities specifically designed for children. For details, look for leaflets in galleries around town or, for a comprehensive directory of buildings involved in the scheme, send an A4 envelope with 41p in stamps on it and £1.50 in stamps inside, a couple of months in advance, to: London Open House, PO Box 25361, London NW5 1GY. / www.londonopenhouse.org.

National Trust Free Entry Day

There's generally a charge to enter National Trust properties (except for members), but on one day a year many properties are open free of charge. Needless to say, if you value tranquillity, this is probably not the best time to go. The Trust does not generally advertise the date – for fear of attracting crowds of people who can perfectly well afford to pay – so you'll have to keep your ear to the ground.

/ www.nationaltrust.org.uk.

Raising of the Thames Barrier SE18

Unity Way   (020) 8854 1373

Canute was wrong – you can hold back the tide, but only by spending half a billion pounds on a great river barrier, designed to protect central London from the ever-growing risk of flooding. The Thames Barrier (see also, South London) is a miracle of modern engineering (completed in 1982). Once a year (usually in September or October) there is an all-day test and the massive steel gates are either raised or dropped against the high tide. There are also tests each month, but these take place as early in the morning as tides permit and (because it involves closing a working river) for as short a period as possible. Call the Visitor Centre for details. / BR: Charlton; café.

Thames Festival

Victoria Embankment and South Bank by OXO Tower
(020) 7928 8998

From Frost Fairs to GLC Thames Days, London's river has long been a natural focal point for pageantry and celebrations. The Thames Festival begins from Victoria Embankment, with a spectacular processional of over 2,500 illuminated sculptures and lanterns, which represent the effort of school children and community groups throughout London. The procession ends at the Royal National Theatre with a magnificent fireworks display on the river. Call the Thames Festival Trust for date and time details. / www.thamesfestival.org; Tube: Waterloo, Westminster.

October

Diwali

Funfairs and fireworks take place in Ealing and Hounslow in October to celebrate the Hindu and Sikh festival of light. Check press for details. Local councils often organise festivals.

Punch & Judy Festival WC2

Covent Garden   (020) 7836 9136

The first Sunday of October sees a plethora of Punch and Judy shows, and their continental equivalents – Polichinelle (France), Kasper (Germany) and Pulcinella (Italy). / Tube: Leicester Square.

Southwark Festival*

(020) 7403 7400

Making full use of Southwark's river frontage (which stretches from Tower Bridge to the Millennium footbridge) and unusual venues (including the chapel of Guy's Hospital), the festival's fortnight of events ranges from street theatre and concerts in Southwark Cathedral to historical lectures about the area's past inhabitants and a food fair in Borough Market. Much of the programme is free (both indoor and outdoor events); call or check the website for other events held earlier in the year. / www.southwarkfestival.org.uk; Tube: Southwark, London Bridge, Borough.

Events

State Opening of Parliament
If you want to see the Queen wearing a crown and riding in a gilded coach, the only annual opportunity to do so is the State Opening of Parliament (usually in October). Her Majesty rides from Buckingham Palace to Westminster to deliver the Queen's Speech (which sets out the Government's legislative plans for the forthcoming year, and is, in fact, written by the Prime Minister) and then returns to her palace. There are accompanying gun salutes at Green Park and the Tower of London. As an event, it's not hugely well attended, and offers possibly the best 'royal-watching' opportunity of the year.
/ www.parliament.uk/parliament/guide/maopen.htm; Tube: Westminster.

Trafalgar Day Parade WC2
Trafalgar Sq
A commemoration service for Nelson's 1805 victory at Trafalgar takes place on the nearest Sunday to 21 October. Wreaths are laid at Nelson's Column by over 500 Sea Cadets.
/ Tube: Leicester Square, Charing Cross.

November

Fireworks Night
The annual remembrance of the failure of the Gunpowder plot (when Guy Fawkes and his merry men attempted, in 1605, to blow up monarch, lords and commoners assembled at Westminster) is celebrated with a huge number of bonfire and firework parties of all sizes all over London. Parties take place on November 5 and, if it falls mid-week, the weekends before and after. The larger events are widely advertised on posters and in local newspapers.

Lord Mayor's Show
The Lord Mayor's Show has taken place – plague permitting – in some form in most years since 1215. It celebrates the annual presentation of the new Lord Mayor of London to the Queen's Justices. This formerly took place at Westminster, but now involves a rather shorter journey to the Royal Courts of Justice in the Strand. The show takes place on the second Saturday of November, and begins at the Guildhall at 11am with a one-and-a-half-mile long procession, which includes 60 floats, 20 bands and about 6,000 people. The centrepiece of the procession is the Lord Mayor's gilded, c18 coach (housed for the rest of the year in the Museum of London, see also), pulled by six shire horses. This is a great traditional Londoners' day out – a whole day's entertainment is provided, ending with a firework display over the Thames – and about a quarter of a million people attend annually. Many City attractions, generally closed at weekends, open on the day of the show.
/ www.lordmayorsshow.org; Tube: Bank.

RAC London to Brighton Veteran Car Run

*Saturday 14 November 1896 was a great day in the history
of British motoring – for the first time it was legal to proceed
at more than 4mph and without being preceded by a man with
a red flag. Ever since (war years excepted) horseless carriages
have taken part in an annual celebration of automobile
'Emancipation'. The spectacle now attracts over a million
spectators each year. The Run – it is NOT a race – takes place
on the first Sunday in November, leaving Hyde Park at 7.30am,
and progressing via Westminster (7.35am) and Lambeth Town
Hall (7.45am) to Madeira Drive, Brighton, where the
frontrunners arrive around 10.30am. Only cars built before
1905 are eligible to take part, and competitors come from all
over the world.* / www.vccofgb.co.uk/lbpage.htm; Tube: Hyde Park Corner.

Remembrance Sunday SW1

Whitehall
*The Sunday nearest to 11 November sees the most sober, and
the most moving, large-scale event of the year. Just after 11am,
the Queen and representatives of the government and the
Commonwealth lay wreaths of Flanders poppies on the
Cenotaph to commemorate those who gave their lives in war.
After the short service, the tone becomes a little lighter as the
veterans march past.* / Tube: Embankment, Charing Cross, Westminster.

Christmas Parade

*American-style parade with 2,000 participants including
dancers, clowns, marching bands and floats that takes place
from Berkeley Square, Oxford Street and Regent Streets to
Piccadilly Circus, on one Sunday in late November.*
/ Tube: Oxford Circus, Piccadilly Circus, Bond Street.

December

Christmas Lights

*The heartland of London's shopping – Oxford Street, Regent
Street and Bond Street – achieves charming results with its
Christmas lights (although in past years, commercial
sponsorship of the illuminations made them somewhat less
appealing). Carnaby Street also joins in, usually with some fairly
avant-garde variations on the festive theme. The illuminations
are given a celebrity 'switch on' in November, and they are
there to be admired until Twelfth Night. An evening visit to this
part of town also permits some vigorous window-shopping at
Selfridges and the other stores of Oxford Street, and Hamleys
and Liberty on Regent Street. Fortnum & Mason on Piccadilly
usually puts on a good display as well (and its windows are
worth a special look at any time of year). Do note that, in
the run-up to Christmas, the whole of the West End can be
surprisingly crowded well after the shops have closed.*
/ Tube: Marble Arch, Oxford Circus, Bond Street, Piccadilly Circus.

Events

Christmas Tree WC2

Trafalgar Sq

The great Christmas Tree in Trafalgar Square, decorated with its bright white lamps, is an annual gift from the people of Oslo to the people of London. There are regular carol concerts around the tree. / Tube: Charing Cross.

Spitalfields Winter Festival* E1

Christ Church, Commercial St   Hotline (020) 7377 1362

See the Summer Festival (June) for details. The Winter Festival – apart from the obvious Christmas theme and carol singing – is very similar. / Times: church, Mon-Fri 12pm-2.30pm & Sun between services; festival, details from hotline; www.spitalfieldsfestival.org.uk; Tube: Shoreditch, Liverpool Street, Aldgate East.

New Year's Eve

Packing yourself into Trafalgar Square WC2 is traditionally the way to see in the New Year in London. Those who do not like crowds should definitely stay away, and even those who do should think twice – as midnight approaches the drunken crush can be absolutely unbearable and it can be so crowded as to be impossible to get into the Square itself. Getting home is, unusually, free of charge as London Transport operates its annual (usually sponsored) offer of free transport throughout the capital, with the tubes running well past midnight. Alternatively, you could spend the evening spanning two hemispheres – the Greenwich and Docklands Festival (see above for details and website) organise a free New Year's Eve event called First Night, with fireworks and street entertainments, centred on Greenwich town centre.

Entertainments

Radio & Television

London's position as a great centre of music and broadcasting means that there's a huge amount of entertainment of every kind being produced – from classical concerts to game-shows. And it's there just for the asking, as being a member of the studio audience is invariably free.

Below, we give details of organisations which produce concerts and shows, both for radio and TV. If you really want to see a particular programme (which is not produced by one of these companies) there's no substitute for tracking down the production company and asking how it allocates tickets.

Radio – BBC W12

Audience Services, PO Box 3000, London W12 7RJ
Recorded information (020) 8576 1227

Radio shows tend to be scheduled only about six weeks ahead, so audience tickets are often available at short notice. You might listen to a recording of The Now Show *or* Brain of Britain. *The recorded information service tells you what's on offer and they will, on request, put your name on a mailing list (but currently, there is only one for radio comedy) and you will be kept up to date with what's available in that type of entertainment. There's something for almost all tastes, from classical concerts, via easy listening, to quiz programmes. Radio shows are mainly recorded at the BBC Radio Theatre at Broadcasting House W1 and concerts are usually at the Maida Vale Studios, Delaware Road W9. / www.bbc.co.uk/tickets.*

Television – BBC W12

Audience Services, Room 309, Design Building,
Television Centre, London W12 7RJ   (020) 8576 1227

There's a huge choice of comedies, variety shows, quiz programmes and debates you can watch being recorded during the afternoon and evening. Ring to check there is a series coming up and that the BBC makes the programme you want to see (some are filmed by separate production companies – Have I Got News For You *is made by Hat Trick Productions, for example, see also) and ask for information about what's currently on offer or send an SAE to Audience Services to receive a print version. People drop out at short notice so it is worth trying for shows happening in the near future. Singles and parties are welcome, and this is an ideal outing for all ages that costs no more than the coach hire. Children aged under 14 are not generally admitted. Further information is also available via email: tv.ticket.unit@bbc.co.uk. / www.bbc.co.uk.*

Television – Channel 5
Channel 5 Duty Office, PO Box 55, Nottingham NG1 5HE
(0345) 050505
*Companies making programmes for the newest of England's
terrestrial TV stations may advertise for audience members, for
example in* Time Out. *Channel 5 does not have a mailing list
but you can keep up-to-date with what's available via the Duty
Office.* / www.channel5.co.uk.

Television – Hat Trick Productions
(020) 7287 1598
Most famous for Have I Got News for You *and* Who's Line
is it Anyway?, *this independent company also made* Drop
the Dead Donkey *and* Father Ted. *There's no mailing list
and it seems regulars call the ticketline every six weeks or so
to check availability (tickets are also available from a website).
You do stand a chance of getting tickets for your favourite
show, but only if you start trying several months in advance.
Generally, the minimum age for children attending a show is
15. Most recording is at the London Studios on the South Bank.*
/ www.hattrick.co.uk.

Television – LWT SE1
London Studios, Upper Ground   (020) 7620 1620
This ITV company, which produces shows including Blind Date
*at their studios on the South Bank, runs a mailing list for
people wishing to apply for tickets. Write or telephone to
put your name on the list. (The website also lists other ITV
companies, whose shows may also be filmed in London, such
as* The Pepsi Chart*). /* www.itv.co.uk.

Music

Most of the major arts centres offer free foyer music
(often of very high quality) on a regular basis. Details are
given under the entries for the respective venues – see the
Royal Festival Hall and the **Royal National Theatre**
(South), the **Royal Opera House** (Central) and the
Barbican (City). Other places listed which offer regular
free music include **Westminster Abbey** (Central),
St Mary Abbots (West), Christchurch Spitalfields (City)
and the Union Chapel (North).

A major centre of popular, modern music, the capital
boasts a number of world-renowned clubs and music
venues. While the majority, unfortunately, charge entrance
fees for performances, there are still quite a number of
places to hear rock, dance, jazz or world music for free.
Major music and book stores – HMV, Virgin Records,
Borders and Tower Records – host live performances
and album release concerts from time to time.

Entertainments

To hear free live shows at music venues, Mon or Tue evenings are generally the best bet. In addition, on many nights, free admission can be had by arriving early in the evening, say, before 9pm.

One of the most reliable options for seeing live music is in bars and pubs, which offer intimate settings for performances. A popular pub event is the 'open mic night', in which any sort of aspiring artist, from folk singer to diva, can take the stage. These showcases provide a good opportunity to hear a wide range of musical tastes, and perhaps even see a future star. A number of periodicals, such as *Time Out* (which specifically notes free evenings), list the musical happenings of the capital. Better yet, check your 'local' for upcoming gigs.

City Music
There is music in one of the many churches of the City almost every lunchtime – almost all concerts begin between 1pm and 1.15pm and generally last no more than an hour. A useful monthly publication, City Events, *available from the City of London Information Centre by St Paul's, gives advance details. Alternatively, if you arrive at the centre by 12.40pm you should have time to locate the concert of your choice and walk to the appropriate church.*

The top time of year for City music is during the City of London Festival (see also) in late June/early July.

The Corporation of London also presents a series of band concerts through the summer at four locations (Finsbury Circus, Tower Place, Royal Exchange Forecourt and St Paul's Cathedral Steps) from noon to 2pm on Wed and Thu (Jun – Sep) – you can get a leaflet from the Information Centre.
/ Tube: Bank, St Paul's.

Events in the Royal Parks
(020) 7298 2000
Most of the Royal Parks (Hyde, Regent's, St James's, Green, Greenwich and Richmond, and Kensington Gardens) have music, and other events, on a regular basis. It's well worth sending an A5 SAE to Old Police House, Hyde Park, London W2 2UH (tel (020) 7298 2000), asking for a Summer Entertainment Programme, or check the website. Events of interest to adults include theatrical and operatic productions, dancing demonstrations and guided nature and gardening tours of the parks. For children, there are circus acts and puppet shows. / www.royalparks.co.uk.

Guildhall School of Music & Drama* EC2
Barbican, Silk St   (020) 7382 7192   5–1C
Opera, jazz, ensemble, contemporary music... performances, most of which are free, take place at the School, at the Barbican, and elsewhere, lunchtimes and evenings. Call for the termly programme which gives full details. / www.gsmd.ac.uk; Tube: Moorgate, Barbican.

Music colleges

London boasts some of the finest music colleges in the world and, to those who enjoy classical music they represent an extremely fertile source of free entertainment.

All the schools listed give three or four concerts or recitals a week during their term times. The most popular performances tend to be the larger ones – those with symphony orchestras or pieces with a large chorus – of which there may be five or so in a term at a given school.

Royal Academy of Music NW1

Marylebone Rd   (020) 7873 7300   2–1A
Details of some ten free events a week are listed in the termly Diary of Events (available from the box office on the number given). In general, lunchtime concerts take place Tue-Thu at 1.05pm in the foyer, while early-evening concerts take place on Tue at 5.05pm in the Duke's Hall. In addition, there are various other evening concerts, showcasing classical, jazz and chamber music. New in 2001 is a chamber music series called Free on Fridays *which is designed to show off the Academy's best performers. The concerts begin at 1.05pm and last about an hour.* / www.ram.ac.uk; Tube: Baker Street; café.

Royal College of Music SW7

Prince Consort Rd   (020) 7589 3643 ext 4380   3–1B
Most of the performances are given at the college, just behind the Royal Albert Hall, although quite a number are held at other venues around the capital. For example, at 1.10pm on Fridays during term time, a concert is given at the imposing Church of St Mary Abbots in the centre of Kensington (tube: Kensington High Street). Lunchtime concerts (Mon-Thu, beginning at 1.05pm) take place variously in the Recital Hall, the Concert Hall and St Mary Abbots, so check the website or ring for details. / www.rcm.ac.uk; Tube: (College) South Kensington.

Royal Opera House* WC2

Covent Garden   (020) 7304 4000 (Box office)   2–2D
A multi-million pound refurbishment has given the Royal Opera House several new 'spaces', one of which is the Linbury Studio Theatre, where free chamber music concerts are given on Mondays at 1pm. Visitors to the Opera House are also able to see the recently-refurbished foyer areas and view permanent displays and temporary exhibitions situated around the building. (Some areas may be unavailable if events are taking place during the day.)

A great opportunity to get a taste of opera or ballet for free is the BP Opera and Ballet in the Piazza, a rolling programme featuring three live relays annually – performances happening within the opera house are broadcast live to the masses seated in the market square (weather permitting). Check the website for further details. / Times: Opera House from 10am; Vilar Floral Hall 10am-3pm; www.royalopera.org; Tube: Covent Garden.

Entertainments

Shell LSO Music Scholarship Final
Royal Festival Hall   (020) 7960 4242
(Royal Festival Hall Box Office)
*The £6,000 Shell LSO Music Scholarship is one of the
most prestigious prizes available to young musicians. The
competition final is held in late June/early July each year
and involves the LSO performing selected movements with
the four competitors. It's a very enjoyable event if you prefer
listening to classical music in a very informal atmosphere.
Tickets are allocated on a first-come, first-served basis by the
Royal Festival Hall Box Office – contact the number given,
or for more information call the LSO Scholarship Administrator
on (01223) 501709.* / www.lso.co.uk/aboutthelso/shell.htm;
Tube: Waterloo, Embankment.

Trinity College of Music W1
11 Mandeville Place   (020) 7935 5773   2–1A
*Most concerts and recitals take place around 1pm in the
Barbirolli Lecture Hall or in the nearby Hinde Street church.
In addition to performances, there are occasional musical
competitions and large-scale concerts. A Diary of Events
can be obtained from the number given.*
/ www.tcm.ac.uk; Tube: Bond Street.

Central London

Introduction

The fact that Central London is at the ceremonial and governmental heart of Britain – comprising as it does the **Houses of Parliament**, **Westminster Abbey**, **Buckingham Palace** and 10 Downing Street – provides an almost unequalled range of famous historic attractions. The Abbey and Parliament can be visited, but only with a degree of planning.

Another major theme is art and antiquities – this area contains some of the most significant museums and art galleries in the world. In the mega-league are the **British Museum**, the **National Gallery** and **Tate Britain**. There are, however, also smaller attractions with first-rate collections – among these the **Wallace Collection** and **Sir John Soane's Museum** stand out. In addition, the commercial art world provides a huge and ever-changing selection of pictures and objects to view, and the institutions which deal in them have their own special interest and charm. A visit to one of the great auctioneers, **Sotheby's** or **Christie's**, combines art with theatre. (For a guide to the commercial galleries, see Galleries on page 14).

Central London is a window-shopper's paradise, containing as it does most of the UK's top shops – ranging from **Harrods**, Selfridges and **Fortnum & Mason** at the larger end of the scale to the opulent boutiques of **Old Bond Street**, and the charming, small shops in the Regency **Burlington Arcade**. Almost all of the very central areas have sufficient character to justify just strolling around, but **Covent Garden** should be on most lists as it boasts outdoor entertainers and a variety of festivals year-round.

With children, this can be a rather tiring area. There are the sights of course – **Trafalgar Square** and **Eros** can be added to those already mentioned – and there is also the possibility of a trip to **Hamleys**, the world-famous toy shop. Leaving this aside, the top attractions for families are probably **St James's Park** – which is pretty and interesting enough to provide something for everyone – and **Coram's Fields**, a useful amenity for kids in Bloomsbury.

Suggested walks

To orientate yourself within central London, try one of these three interesting walks below – one 'historical', one 'intellectual' and the third 'cultural'.

The first stroll encompasses London's most impressive historical sights. Begin at Trafalgar Square, making sure to dodge the buses and pigeons (not always in that order). To the west stretches Pall Mall. Stroll down this wide avenue, flanked by impressive gentlemen's clubs, until reaching St James's Palace. (If you get there by 11.15am, you can follow the St James's Palace detachment of the Queen's Guard as it marches to Buckingham Palace – this walk is not short of picture opportunities, as the throngs of tourists will attest.) From Buckingham Palace, one is a short distance from the immaculate St. James's Park – one of the oldest royal parks. Enter on the western edge of the park, walking alongside St. James's Park Lake and passing Duck Island. Exit at the southeast corner and follow Great George Street towards Westminster. The Abbey and the Houses of Parliament will soon come into view. From this point, the final stage of the walk begins. Head north along Parliament Street, which becomes Whitehall, past Downing Street, the Horse Guards Parade and finally back to Trafalgar Square.

Our second recommended walk also begins at Trafalgar Square, but moves north, rather than west. Begin by walking up Charing Cross Road. As you pass Leicester Square to your left, and Long Acre to your right, a long literary path unfolds – a book-lover's dream. Along each side of Charing Cross Road until Oxford Street lies almost the full gamut of booksellers – from the niche specialists to the commercial giants – making for an interesting afternoon within the heart of town.

For a less intellectually strenuous jaunt, begin at Leicester Square and head north along Leicester Place to Lisle Street. Immediately, the colourful restaurants, markets and stores of Chinatown are in full view. Move west to Wardour Street and turn right. Gerrard Street on the right is the pedestrianised centre of Chinatown. Head further north up Wardour Street and you will be thrust into the crowded, teeming streets of Soho. Slowly the area becomes a mix of the chic, the colourful and the exotic. Soho and its environs has something for all tastes, from galleries and gay bars, to 'adult' entertainment options and a variety of restaurants. You can move easily in any direction off Wardour Street to explore the secrets of Soho. Perhaps turn left on to Broadwick Street which will lead you to Carnaby Street – the home of swinging '60s London, re-inventing itself once more as a fashion hot-spot after years of being populated with tourist-trap shops. Inevitably, your wanderings will take you to one of the boundaries of Soho – Oxford Street to the north, Regent Street to the west and Charing Cross Road to the east. On all three streets, there are tube stations and bus stops, making a nice end point for your journey.

London Tourist Board SW1

Victoria Station   2–4B
The main outlet of London's tourist board is within Victoria Station. (See entry on page 11) / www.londontown.com; Tube: Victoria.

Indoor attractions

Alfred Dunhill SW1

48 Jermyn St   (020) 7290 8622   2–3B
Jermyn Street, London's most discreet shopping thoroughfare, boasts the headquarters of one of the more successful brand names in the international luxury branded goods market. The Alfred Dunhill Museum (in the basement of the refurbished shop) houses examples of motoring accessories, jewellery, watches, handbags and smoking items manufactured by the company over the last century. Give 48 hours notice and you can arrange a guided tour. / Times: Mon-Sat 9.30am (Sat 10am)-6pm; Tube: Green Park, Piccadilly Circus.

Architectural Association WC1

34-36 Bedford Sq   (020) 7636 0974;
recorded info (020) 7887 4111   2–1C
For anyone with an interest in architecture, the Association offers a rich and varied programme of afternoon and evening lectures. There are also project exhibitions by contemporary architects and students in the Exhibition Gallery and Photo Library throughout the year. Call to find out times of lectures. / Times: Mon-Sat 10am-7pm (Sat 3pm); www.aaschool.ac.uk; Tube: Tottenham Court Road.

Architecture Centre, Royal Institute of British Architects (RIBA) W1

66 Portland Pl   (020) 7580 5533   2–1B
The Architecture Centre is an international showcase for today and the future, and focuses on awards and competitions. However, it also shows some eccentric exhibitions. (See also Heinz Gallery, RIBA.) / Times: Mon-Sat 8am-6pm (Tue 9pm); www.architecture.com; Tube: Great Portland Street, Regents Park; café.

Architecture Foundation SW1

The Economist Building, 30 Bury St
(020) 7253 3334   2–3B
This body is "dedicated to the display and discussion of contemporary architecture and the built environment in a way that appeals to the public". In addition to an exhibition programme, it holds a series of forums on architectural and urban planning questions, to which the public is invited. The building was refurbished in late-2000. / Times: Tue-Sun 12pm-6pm; www.architecturefoundation.org.uk; Tube: Green Park.

Ben Uri Art Society N3
The Manor House, 80 East End Rd   (020) 8349 5724
The Society has been housed in temporary accommodation since 1997, but finally seems to have found its own exhibition space. The collection includes more than 800 works by Jewish artists including Bomberg, Auerbach, Epstein and Kitaj. Further information of when, what and where is available via the world wide web or e-mail: benuri@ort.org. / www.benuri.ort.org.

BOC Museum WC1
Association of Anaesthetists of GB & Ireland, 9 Bedford Sq
(020) 7631 1650   2–1C
The museum is home to one of the largest collections of early and contemporary anaesthetic equipment in the world. Each year a special topic is presented, taken from over 5,000 items in the collection. / Times: by telephone appt with the Archivist; www.aagbi.org; Tube: Goodge Street, Tottenham Court Road.

Bonhams SW7
Montpelier St   (020) 7393 3900   3–1C
If you're in the market for a fine and rare cased self-opening 20-bore Royal Brevis side-lock ejector sporting gun by Holland & Holland or a brilliant-cut diamond heart-shaped pendant – or, as a reader of this book just want a look at such items, Bonhams art auction may be the place for you. / Times: Mon-Fri 9am-4:30pm, Sun 11am-3pm; www.bonhams.com; Tube: Knightsbridge.

British Cartoon Centre WC1
7 Brunswick Centre, Bernard St   (020) 7278 7172   2–1D
The British Cartoon Centre (formerly the National Museum of Cartoon Art) displays all forms of cartoon art, from stick figures to 3-dimensional drawings, with various exhibitions during the year in its two galleries. A recent exhibition focused on the work of Charles Schulz, creator of Charlie Brown. Entrance is free, but donations are appreciated. / Times: Mon-Fri 12pm-8pm; www.cartooncentre.com; Tube: Russell Square.

British Museum WC1
Great Russell St   (020) 7636 1555   2–1C
Six million visitors a year can't be wrong – this august neo-classical building (Robert Smirke, 1823-52) is London's leading attraction – free or otherwise. It does, after all, house what is arguably the world's greatest collection of antiquities. The museum is currently undergoing a series of renovations and redevelopments, in preparation for its 250th anniversary in 2003. The greatest of these is the Great Court, which has transformed the previously-hidden inner courtyard into one of London's greatest public spaces. The two-acre square, with the world-famous Round Reading Room at its centre, has been enclosed by a spectacular glass roof.

Particular strengths of the collection include Egyptian antiquities, coins and medals, the collections relating to Greek and Roman civilisation (especially, of course, the marbles from the Parthenon), clocks, and prints and drawings. No-one could possibly take in the whole museum in a day – just to pass by all the exhibits would apparently require a walk of some two and a half miles – so it's probably worth deciding on a section of particular interest and trying to make sense of that. From Mon-Fri, the museum's experts give gallery talks at 11.15am and lectures at 1.15pm. Free daily 'eyeOpener' tours, which focus on different areas of the museum, run all day and last approximately 50 minutes. There are many interesting temporary exhibitions (mostly free of charge) and there are regular talks and films, and even occasional art workshops for children. / *Times: Mon-Sat 10am-5pm, Sun 10am-5.30pm; www.thebritishmuseum.ac.uk; Tube: Russell Square, Tottenham Court Road, Holborn; restaurant & café.*

Burlington Arcade W1

Between Piccadilly and Burlington Gardens 2–2B

This Regency shopping arcade is perhaps the most timeless place in London for window-shopping. Top-hatted beadles maintain standards – no running, no singing, no carrying large parcels, etc – leaving you in perfect serenity to survey the displays in the windows of the small, elegant shops, some of which still sell hand-made luxury goods. / *Times: Mon-Sat 9am-5.30pm; www.burlington-arcade.co.uk; Tube: Green Park, Piccadilly Circus.*

Canada House SW1

Trafalgar Sq (entrance on Cockspur St)
(020) 7258 6600   2–2C

Overlooking Trafalgar Square, the home of the Canadian High Commission (restored in 1998) was built by Sir Robert Smirke, who also designed the British Museum. Visitors are free to tour the decorative premises. There is an especially stunning view of Whitehall, towards Parliament Square, from the third floor's elliptical windows. There are regular themed exhibitions, at which visitors can obtain information about everything Canadian, from the arts to history. There is free internet service for those wishing to use the computers to do any kind of research on Canada and – for Canadians only – to check e-mail. / *Times: Mon-Fri 10am-6pm; www.dfait-maeci.gc.ca/london; Tube: Charing Cross.*

Christie's SW1

8 King St   (020) 7839 9060   2–3B

The two great international auction-houses (the other, of course, is Sotheby's, which has its own entry, see also) both originated in London. Christie's has been helping collectors build up, and, in later generations dispose of, great collections of pictures and furniture since 1766.

Except for the very grandest sales (to which admission is restricted to those who have bought catalogues), you are welcome to have a look at the goods to be auctioned in the four days before the sale and, indeed, to attend the auction itself – one of the best free shows in town. / Times: Mon-Fri 9.30am-4.30pm (Tue 8pm), Sun 2pm-4.30pm; www.christies.com; Tube: Green Park.

City Yeomanry Museum WC2
10 Stone Buildings, Lincolns Inn   (020) 7405 8112   5–2A
A small museum whose permanent exhibit includes uniforms, medals and equipment of the Inns of Court Regiment and the City of London Yeomanry. / Times: by appt only Mon-Fri 8:30am-4:30pm; www.army.mod.uk/ceremonialandheritage/museums/; Tube: Chancery Lane.

Contemporary Applied Art W1
2 Percy St   (020) 7436 2344   2–1C
At Britain's largest gallery specialising in the exhibition and sale of contemporary crafts you find jewellery, fine metalwork, ceramics, wood, textiles, furniture, glass and paper. Seven exhibitions are held a year – they are free to attend but, as everything is for sale, your visit could turn out to be expensive! / Times: Mon-Sat 10.30am-5.30pm; www.caa.org.uk; Tube: Goodge Street, Tottenham Court Road.

Courtauld Gallery* WC2
Somerset House, Strand   (020) 7848 2526   2–2D
This world-renowned gallery features a rich collection of works – from the Renaissance to the Impressionists. Included in the collection is Manet's Bar at the Folies-Bergères and Van Gogh's Self-Portrait with Bandaged Ear. The gallery benefits from its link to the Courtauld Institute of Fine Art which holds an art history lecture series on Tuesday evenings. Ring (020) 7848 2777 for further information. A visit to the gallery makes a relaxing stop after lunch in nearby Victoria Embankment Gardens. (See also Somerset House and Gilbert Collection.) / Times: Mon 10am-2pm; www.courtauld.ac.uk; Tube: Temple.

Dickens & Jones
Personal Beauty Studio W1
224-244 Regent St   (020) 7287 4947   2–2B
A visit to this team of independent make-up and skin care artists, headed up by Paul Herrington, former lead make-up artist of Space NK, will result in an individual beauty profile. You can revel in the attention as the team works to find the best make-up look for you that works with your skin. Appointments can last up to 90 minutes, but you must prepare far in advance – the waiting list is currently three months. Unsurprisingly, there may well be pressure for you to buy the products after your consultation. / Times: by appt only Mon-Sat 10.15am-4.30pm (Thu 5.30pm); Tube: Oxford Circus.

Central London

Flaxman Gallery WC1
University College, Gower St   (020) 7679 7700   2–1C
John Flaxman (1755-1826) was a pre-eminent name in the emergence of neo-classicism in England. In 1810, he was appointed the first Professor of Sculpture at the Royal Academy. The gallery displays many of the plaster models from which marble sculptures were subsequently made.
/ Times: Mon-Fri 8.45am-10.30am (Fri 7pm), Sat 9.30am-4.30pm; www.ucl.ac.uk; Tube: Warren Street, Goodge Street.

Fortnum & Mason W1
181 Piccadilly   (020) 7734 8040   2–2B
The royal grocers (established on this site in 1707) have all the accoutrements you could possibly desire of such an establishment – plush red carpets, glittering chandeliers and assistants in tailcoats. The shop has particularly impressive displays of its famous produce, both in the grand ground floor sales area, expanded in 1998, and in the Piccadilly windows. The external clock is a well-known landmark – see the outdoor section. / Times: Mon-Sat 10am-6.30pm (closed bank holidays); www.fortnumandmason.com; Tube: Green Park, Piccadilly Circus.

Foyle's WC2
113-119 Charing Cross Rd   (020) 7437 5660   2–2C
You can potter happily for hours in this establishment – Britain's largest bookshop in terms of number of titles – which carries a copy of almost every book in print, however esoteric. After many years in decline, there is every sign that this may once again become one of London's best bookshops as well as one of the biggest. There is also an art gallery, (020) 7440 3245, on the second floor, with changing exhibitions.
/ Times: Mon-Sat 9am-7.30pm, Sun 12pm-6pm; www.foyles.co.uk; Tube: Tottenham Court Road.

Gilbert Collection* WC2
Somerset House, Strand   (020) 7420 9400   2–2D
Sir Arthur Gilbert, a Briton who made his fortune in the US, has chosen the old country as the recipient of his intriguing collection, whose highlights include gold snuff boxes and Italian mosaics. The display, in impressive former cellars of Somerset House, also includes furniture, silver, clocks and portrait miniatures. (See also Somerset House and Courtauld Gallery.)
/ Times: Mon 10am-2pm; www.gilbert-collection.org.uk; Tube: Temple; café.

Grant Museum of Zoology & Comparative Anatomy WC1

Biology Department (Darwin Building), University College, Gower St (020) 7677 2647 2–1C

This natural history museum holds some 35,000 specimens which range across the animal kingdom, from an aardvark and gorillas to sloths and a quagga (an extinct type of zebra) – there are skeletons, specimens in jars and real stuffed animals. Although it is primarily a resource for education, the museum is open to anyone by appointment and is popular with photographers and artists. School groups are also welcome.
/ Times: Wed & Fri 1pm-5pm & by appt: call Helen Chatterjee (e-mail zoology.museum@ucl.ac.uk); www.ucl.ac.uk/biology/museum; Tube: Euston, Euston Square, Warren Street or Goodge Street.

Grays Antique Market W1

58 Davies St (020) 7629 7034 2–2B

There are few destinations in London which offer rare gems and minerals, antique rifles, Islamic Art and the river Tyburn flowing through the basement! These two grand Edwardian buildings, off Bond Street, are home to an antiques market with over 200 stalls and shops (including a large antiquarian book dealer), offering the usual assortment of the useful and useless. However, the true speciality of the place is the monthly themed exhibitions – subjects vary widely, from Beatles memorabilia to extensive and ever-popular erotica collections. / Times: Mon-Fri 10am-6pm; www.egrays.co.uk; Tube: Bond Street.

Great Ormond Street Hospital for Children WC1

Peter Pan Gallery, 55 Great Ormond St
(020) 7405 9200 2–1D

An exhibition relating to the history of this famous children's hospital, founded in 1852, is housed in a neighbouring Georgian town house. Exhibits include photographs and ephemera. Since 1929 the hospital has received the copyright proceeds from sales of J M Barrie's Peter Pan (extended in perpetuity in the UK by a unique Act of Parliament in 1987 when the copyright expired), and there are letters from the author as well as copies of the book in a number of languages.
/ Times: by appt, Mon-Fri 9.30am-4.30pm; www.gosh.org; Tube: Russell Square, Holborn, Euston.

Hamleys W1

188 Regent St (020) 7494 2000 2–2B

At Christmas it's unbearably crowded, but all year round, this is the number one destination on any child's tour of London – the world's largest toyshop. Highlights from the seven jam-packed floors include moving displays, talking books, a haunted staircase and a huge model railway. / Times: Mon-Sat 10am-7pm (sometimes longer hours), Sun 12pm-6pm; www.hamleys.co.uk; Tube: Piccadilly Circus, Oxford Circus; café.

Harrods SW1

Knightsbridge   (020) 7730 1234   3–1D

Europe's most famous department store works very hard to ensure there is always something new to see in its 25 acres of sales space. First-time visitors should not miss the Food Halls, with their intriguing décor and amazing arrangements of produce, but it is the sheer scale of the whole building and the opulence of some of the goods which are probably the main attractions. Special exhibitions are sometimes organised in the ground floor Central Hall. Harrods is a little sensitive about its role as a free tourist attraction – security guards may not allow large parties or people with big bags, dress should be appropriate and photography is not allowed. / Times: Mon-Sat 10am-7pm; www.harrods.com; Tube: Knightsbridge.

Harvey Nichols SW1

Knightsbridge   (020) 7235 5000   3–1D

Harvey Nichols is a smaller, more intimate department store than its better-known Knightsbridge neighbour and not, therefore, quite as suited to sightseeing. The particularly innovative window displays are always interesting, though, and the glamorous foodie complex on the fifth floor is worth a look for the sheer improbability of its Dan Dare-style architecture and location. / Times: Mon-Sat 10am-7pm (Wed, Thu & Fri 8pm), Sun 12pm-6pm; www.harveynichols.com; Tube: Knightsbridge.

Houses of Parliament SW1

(020) 7219 4272   2–3C

No visitor will wish to miss the sight of the Palace of Westminster, with its famous clock tower (whose bell is known as Big Ben). There has been a royal palace here since c11, but after a disastrous fire in 1835, the building was reconstructed in neo-Gothic style to the designs of Charles Barry and Augustus Pugin.

The building is not generally open to the public, but if you want to see the fine interior – or our ancient democracy at work – there are two ways of going about it. One is to arrange to go on a tour and the other is to watch a debate – in the Commons or Lords (from one of the Strangers' Galleries) or in a Commons committee. Dealing with the former first, UK citizens wishing to have a tour must apply to their MP in writing, and should do so well in advance. Citizens of other countries may apply, in writing, to the Public Information Office of the House of Commons (and may be accommodated at shorter notice). Tours of the Palace include the c14 Westminster Hall, where Charles I was tried in 1649. (Tours are usually only available Mon-Thu mornings & Fri afternoons; this varies during parliamentary recesses.)

If you want to watch a debate in progress, the galleries are open to the public. However, priority is given to those with tickets, and the safest course, therefore, to avoid a lengthy queue, is to apply for a ticket, as far in advance as possible, to your MP (or, if you are not a UK citizen, to your embassy or High Commission). Impromptu visitors have a good chance of gaining admission (unless the subject of debate is very controversial) later on in the day – sittings usually go on until 10pm, and sometimes beyond – or on Fri.

If you're planning any visit to Parliament, it's a very good idea to check out your plans with the Public Information Office on the number given. / www.parliament.uk; Tube: Westminster.

Liberty W1
214-220 Regents St   (020) 7734 1234   2–2B
Liberty is one of the most charming and individualistic of London's department stores. It occupies very characterful mock-Tudor premises (built in the '20s, from timbers of men o'war), which are certainly worth a look, especially the creaky staircases. The store's particular strength is house furnishings and it carries many interesting and unusual objects and fabrics, as well as clothing and cosmetics. / Times: Mon-Sat 10am-6.30pm, (Thu 9pm, Fri & Sat 8pm), Sun 12pm-6pm; www.liberty.co.uk; Tube: Oxford Circus.

The Library & Museum of Freemasonry WC2
Great Queen St   (020) 7395 9258   2–2D
If you have always been fascinated by the aura of secrecy of Freemasonry, it may come as a surprise that the Masons are very pleased for you to visit their daunting Grand Temple in Covent Garden. The current monolith was dedicated in 1933, but the site has been associated with Freemasonry for over two centuries. The Library and Museum (with collections of plate, glassware, jewels, regalia and Masonic memorabilia) are open to the public. There are usually hourly tours which include the principal ceremonial rooms and the Grand Temple, but call before you set off. / Times: Mon-Fri 10am-5pm, Sat by appt only; www.grandlodge-england.org; Tube: Holborn, Covent Garden.

London Brass Rubbing Centre* WC2
The Crypt, St Martin-in-the-Fields Church
(020) 7930 906   2–2C
This charming workshop area is just off the crypt café. Visitors can view brass rubbings, many of which feature knights in armour ready for the joust, and watch modern-day enthusiasts taking rubbings. The exhibition is free, but there is a fee to make a rubbing. / Times: 10am (Sun 12pm)-6pm; Tube: Charing Cross; café.

London Scottish Regimental Museum SW1

95 Horseferry Rd   (020) 7630 1639   2–4C

The collection covers the Regiment's uniforms and equipment since its formation in 1859. Exhibits include medals (the regiment has three VCs to its credit), the three war memorials in the Drill Hall, badges, an indexed record of previous members as well as hundreds of photos documenting the history of the Regiment. / Times: by telephone appt Mon-Fri 9am-4pm; www.londonscottish.org.uk; Tube: St James's Park.

National Gallery WC2

Trafalgar Sq   (020) 7747 2885   2–2C

One of the world's great galleries of Western European paintings, from the late c13 to the early c20 – Giotto to Picasso. What distinguishes it is the balance of its collection across all of the schools, with practically no great master unrepresented. The Sainsbury Wing (1991) houses the earliest works from 1260 to 1510 (including Botticelli, Bellini and Raphael), and the rest of the collection progresses chronologically through the West Wing (Michelangelo, Holbein, Titian), the North Wing (Rubens, Velázquez, Rembrandt) and the East Wing (Gainsborough, Turner, Constable, Monet, van Gogh), up to 1900. Daily tours of the collection take place (Mon-Sat), at 11.30am & 2.30pm (also Wed at 6pm), according to the season, and there are lectures or films about artists or schools of painting at 1pm (Tue-Fri). Every Wed evening, student musicians from the Royal College of Music perform in the Central Hall – for information, pick up a copy of The National Gallery News. If you prefer to let your fingers do the walking (or have a child, of any age, to amuse), don't miss the Micro Gallery Computer Information Room, a great resource for research. There is a charge for some special exhibitions. Note that the cloakrooms here won't keep packages or bags. / Times: Mon-Sun 10am-6pm (Wed 9pm); www.nationalgallery.org.uk; Tube: Charing Cross, Leicester Square, Embankment; café & restaurant.

National Portrait Gallery WC2

2 St Martin's Place   (020) 7306 0055   2–2C

This is arguably the most accessible of London's major galleries. Though in most collections it's artistic merit which wins a place, here it's the importance of the subject of the portrait as much as the eminence of the painter, sculptor or photographer (though many of the great British artists are, of course, represented). Almost all of the major figures of English history are recorded, with the contemporary portraiture galleries being the most popular.

The new Ondaatje Wing (opened in May 2000) increased the exhibition space by a half, and includes an IT gallery, lecture theatre, roof-top restaurant (with panoramic city views) and a balcony gallery which specialises in faces from British cultural history. One of the longest escalators in the UK transports visitors up to the top floor, from which they can view the collection chronologically as they return to ground level. On Tue-Thu at 1.10pm (Sat & Sun, 3pm), there is a lecture on some aspect of the collection, and on Fri at 7pm, musicians perform in the Ondaatje Wing. There is also a variety of temporary exhibitions, for some of which there is a charge. / Times: Mon-Sun 10am-6pm (Thu & Fri 9pm); www.npg.org.uk; Tube: Leicester Square, Charing Cross; café & restaurant.

Percival David Foundation of Chinese Art WCI

53 Gordon Sq   (020) 7387 3909   2–1C
The finest collection of Chinese ceramics outside China is not nearly as well known as it deserves. There are approximately 1,700 items of ceramics, reflecting Chinese court taste from the c10 to c18. Particular treasures include a unique pair of blue and white temple vases, whose inscriptions date them to 1351. / Times: Mon-Fri 10.30am-5pm; www.soas.ac.uk/PDF/home.html; Tube: Russell Square, Goodge Street, Euston Square.

Petrie Museum of Egyptian Archaeology WCI

University College, Malet Place   (020) 7679 2000   2–1C
An extraordinary collection of Egyptian antiquities, excavated by the eminent archaeologist Sir Flinders Petrie and his followers since 1884. The collection includes about 80,000 objects, but only about a third of them are on display. The exhibition is organised to illustrate the development of Egyptian culture from Palaeolithic to Roman and Coptic times. There is also a small Syrian Ptolemaic Roman collection, which was excavated by Petrie too. / Times: Tue-Fri 1pm-5pm, Sat. 10am-1pm; www.petrie.ucl.ac.uk; Tube: Warren Street, Goodge Street, Euston Square, Russell Square; café.

Phillips WI

101 New Bond St   (020) 7629 6602   2–2B
It may be a little less well known than Sotheby's and Christie's, but this Mayfair auctioneer offers just the same possibilities of getting close to great (and lesser) works of art. (For an introduction to the auction houses, see Christie's.) Items range from furniture to textiles. Access to viewings and sales is free (as are verbal valuations if you have an item you hope may be of value). / Times: Mon-Fri 8.30am-5pm; www.phillips-auctions.com; Tube: Bond Street.

The Photographers' Gallery WC2
5 & 8 Great Newport St   (020) 7831 1772   2–2C
This large, central space was Britain's first independent gallery devoted to photography. Now over thirty years old, it maintains an ever-changing programme of photographic exhibitions. Details of occasional free tours and forthcoming events are listed in its magazine, GREAT, free in the gallery. The extensive print and book shops are worth a browse, too.
/ Times: Mon-Sun 11am (Sun 12pm)-6pm; www.photonet.org.uk;
Tube: Leicester Square; café.

Poilâne SW1
46 Elizabeth St   (020) 7808 4910   3–2D
Bread from the great Parisian bakery, Poilâne, has almost mythical status in the foodie world. At great expense, ovens mimicking those in the Rue du Cherche-Midi have recently been installed in the heart of Belgravia, and you're welcome to stop by to see them in use. Bread-making tends to have finished by the time they open, but you should catch the croissants – if this weren't a book about doing things for free, we'd suggest you bought one for breakfast! / Times: shop open 7.30am-7.30pm Mon-Sat; www.poilane.fr; Tube: Victoria.

Royal Academy of Arts* W1
Burlington House, Piccadilly   (020) 7300 8000   2–2B
Although there is a charge for all of the exhibitions (of which the most famous is the annual Summer Exhibition), there is no charge for access to the Academy's charming building. In addition, two of its greatest attractions – one architectural, one artistic – are always on view, gratis. The Sackler Galleries extension, built in 1991, is reckoned by many to be one of the most successful modern additions to any period London building (entry to the gallery itself is not free). The glass-sided lift, designed by Norman Foster, by which the galleries are approached, offers a magical journey from the old to the new, and some of the Academy's sculptures are dramatically displayed outside the galleries. At the far end, in its own white space, is displayed the Academy's greatest artistic treasure, the Michelangelo Tondo – the only example in England of the master's sculpture. There are free tours of the early c18 Private Rooms (usually offered three times a week), which are the most characterful part of the Academy – you need to call in advance for details. / Times: 10am-6pm; www.royalacademy.org.uk; Tube: Piccadilly Circus, Green Park; café.

Royal College of Physicians NW1
11 St Andrew's Place   (020) 7935 1174   4–4B
This art-based collection includes exhibits dating back to the c16 – including portraits, slides and photographs, busts, medals and miniatures – chronicling famous medical personalities. The works are of particular interest to people researching family history where relatives have been fellows of the College, and the building (Grade II listed) itself attracts students of architecture. / Times: entry by appt through writing; www.rcplondon.ac.uk; Tube: Regent's Park, Great Portland Street.

Royal Courts of Justice WC2
Strand   (020) 7947 6000   2–2D
Almost all of the most important civil cases in England and Wales end up being tried in this imposing Victorian Gothic building. There are usually at least 50 courts sitting at any one time, so you should be able to find something of interest – trials might cover anything from allocating fault for a serious accident to esoteric 'administrative' law cases, in which people can challenge the Government's exercise of its powers. Children under 16 are not admitted. / Times: Mon-Fri 10am-4pm; Tube: Temple; café.

St Martin-in-the-Fields WC2
Trafalgar Sq   (020) 7766 1100   2–2C
One of the grandest of London's churches – well, its parish does include Buckingham Palace – and a particularly fine sight when floodlit by night. It was designed by James Gibbs and consecrated in 1726. There are concerts every weekday (except Wed & Thu) at 1.05pm – a perfect break from one of the most hectic parts of London or a suitable finale to a visit to the neighbouring National Gallery (see also). Wed & Sun, there is a choral evensong at 5pm. Check the website for periodic free events, which includes a Harvest Festival attended by the 'Pearly' Kings and Queens (first Sunday in October). / Times: 8am-6pm; www.stmartin-in-the-fields.org; Tube: Charing Cross, Embankment; café.

Sir John Soane's Museum* WC2
13 Lincoln's Inn Fields   infoline (020) 7405 2107   2–1D
One of the most extraordinary buildings in the world, this is actually three interconnected townhouses. It was built by the great architect between 1792 and 1824, for his own occupation and as a home for his eclectic collection of treasures. The collection includes important (and sometimes fascinating) artefacts from Egyptian, Greek and Roman civilisations. There are also some pictures, most famously Hogarth's series of paintings, The Rake's Progress and The Election. The greatest attraction, however, is just wandering around this labyrinthine house, which you may do without any charge (though you do have to pay for conducted tours and some special exhibitions). / Times: Tue-Sat 10am-5pm, 1st Tue of month 6pm-9pm; www.soane.org; Tube: Holborn.

Somerset House WC2
Strand   (020) 7845 4600   2–2D
Somerset House (first built in 1547, and since re-modelled many times) is home to several major art collections (see also Courtauld Gallery and Gilbert Collection). On the lower ground floor visitors may watch a (surprisingly) fascinating video which charts the history and many transformations of the building, from a royal palace washed by the River Thames to the office of public bodies such as the Royal Academy and – more recently – the Inland Revenue.

The neo-classical Great Court (which the building surrounds on all sides) is an impressive open space from which to view the building. The new fountain playing there – which springs directly from the granite paving – is London's first major public fountain since Trafalgar Square's was built in 1845. Special choreographed performances occur twice an hour and at night the fountains are lit with fibre-optics to create a dramatic effect. (In the winter months, an ice skating rink sits in the courtyard.) / Times: Mon-Sat 10am-6pm, Sun and bank holiday Mon 12pm-6pm; www.somerset-house.org.uk; Tube: Temple; café.

Sotheby's W1

34-35 New Bond St   (020) 7293 5000   2–2B

Sotheby's is possibly the best known of the great international art auctioneers. Details of access are broadly as for its competitor, Christie's (see also). / Times: Mon-Fri 9am-4.30pm, occasional weekend viewing; www.sothebys.com; Tube: Bond Street, Green Park; café.

Tate Britain SW1

Millbank   (020) 7887 8000;
recorded info (020) 7887 8008   2–4C

Tate Britain occupies a particularly charming Pimlico building overlooking the Thames. Most British artists of any repute, since 1500, are represented: the Blake and Hogarth collections are particularly fine, and the Clore Galleries house the enormous Turner Bequest. (The Tate's international modern art collection now resides in the Tate Modern, see South section.) The displays change, as the gallery is re-hung every year, with different themes that dictate the location of the paintings – they are not restricted by chronology.

The Tate Britain Centenary Development, opening in October 2001, will add six new galleries and fully landscaped grounds to the building. In addition, the Millbank Pier development will link Tate Britain with the Tate Modern.

There are tours of different parts of the collection (lasting about an hour) on weekdays at 11.30am, 2.30pm and 3.30pm and Sat at 3pm, and there are weekly lectures and films – the Tate Events leaflet provides detailed information and times. Almost all of the Tate's attractions are without charge, with the exception of the three large annual shows. / Times: Mon-Sun 10am-5.50pm; www.tate.org.uk; Tube: Pimlico; café.

Twinings WC2

216 Strand   (020) 7353 3511   2–2D

Dating from 1706, the shop of the famous tea company claims to be the oldest in London in its original ownership, and selling the same product. It certainly has a lot of period charm and its compact premises (suitable for small parties only) house a collection illustrating the history of Twinings and its involvement in tea. / Times: Mon-Fri 9.30am-4.45pm & the morning of the Lord Mayor's Show, before & after the events; www.twinings.co.uk; Tube: Temple.

University College Art Collection WC1
Strang Print Room, University College, Gower St
(020) 7679 2540   2–1C
Works on paper are the particular strength of this collection of 8,000 items, which also includes paintings and sculpture. There is no permanent exhibition, and to show off the collection a programme of temporary shows is organised. A catalogue is available and the website contains information about the entire collection. / Times: Wed-Fri 1pm-5pm during term time, at other times by appt; www.collections.ucl.ac.uk; Tube: Warren Street, Euston Square.

Wallace Collection W1
Manchester Sq   (020) 7935 0687   2–1A
Hertford House, an imposing and sumptuous mansion just north of Oxford Street, contains one of the most splendid collections of pictures and artefacts in London, bequeathed to the nation by Lady Wallace in 1897. It has been suggested that Gallery 24, with its pictures by Watteau and Fragonard, houses the finest group of French c18 pictures which can be seen in a single room anywhere. The collection also includes works by Rembrandt, Rubens and Hals (Laughing Cavalier). Extraordinary clocks, Sèvres porcelain and armour are among the other attractions. Free general guided tours are conducted at 1pm on weekdays (also at 11.30am Wed & Sat and 3pm Sun).

To celebrate the museum's centenary, an extensive project of renovations was launched. The central courtyard has been enclosed by an impressive pyramidal glass roof, allowing the re-instatement of marble sculptures and a bronze fountain placed there by Sir Richard Wallace. A restaurant, four galleries, a library and lecture theatre have also been added, making use of the newly-excavated basement. / Times: Mon-Sun 10am (Sun 12pm)-5pm; www.the-wallace-collection.org.uk; Tube: Bond Street; café & restaurant.

Westminster Abbey* SW1
(020) 7222 5152   2–3C
Sadly, in reaction to sheer force of numbers (over 3 million visitors a year), no part of the interior of this great and historic church – whose consecration predated the Invasion of 1066 – is now open gratis to the public. You can always attend a service of course – the choir has a fine reputation – or, if your taste is for something more secular, there is a short weekly organ recital at 5.45pm on Sun. Such visits, however, will provide very limited opportunities to explore the architecture and the many monuments to famous folk.

Admission to the cloisters is free. Rebuilt after a fire in 1298, they would once have been the busiest parts of the Abbey. One can traverse the cloisters to visit the College Garden (donations appreciated), where the Abbey's first Infirmary garden was established in the c11. During July & August, bands play in the garden on Thu between 12.30pm-2pm. / www.westminster-abbey.org; Tube: Westminster, St James's Park.

Central London

Westminster Cathedral* SW1
Victoria St   (020) 7798 9055   2–4C
Completed in 1903, this Byzantine-style Roman Catholic cathedral houses some fine marble work and mosaics, with the sculptures of the 14 Stations of the Cross by Eric Gill being particularly renowned. It is famous for its choir, and services are sung daily except in August. Unfortunately there is a small charge to ascend the campanile (bell tower), which gives a fine view over much of London. Visitors cannot explore while services are in progress. / Times: Mon-Sun 7am (Sat 8am)-7pm; www.westminstercathedral.org.uk; Tube: Victoria.

Westminster City Archive SW1
10 St Ann's St   (020) 7641 5180   2–4C
Most boroughs have an archive, and if you are at all interested in the history of a particular area, make sure to check it out. These can be quite fascinating places, filled with information on all aspects of local life you might never otherwise have considered looking for, and family historians find them a particularly helpful resource. In addition, there are usually exhibitions on aspects of local history. This being Westminster, these particular archives are extensive and are housed in an impressive new building, tucked away behind the Abbey. Over 5 kilometres of shelving hold around 60,000 items – the earliest piece is dated 1256. / Times: Tue-Sat 9.30am-7pm (Wed 9pm, Sat 5pm); www.westminster.gov.uk/el/libarch/archives; Tube: St James's Park.

Outdoor attractions

Buckingham Palace* SW1
(020) 7930 4832   2–3B
This house has been the principal residence of the Sovereign only since Victoria's day. You know if Her Majesty is at home because the royal standard (a red, gold and blue quartered flag, with lions and a harp) replaces the Union Flag on the flagpole. The main façade, facing the Mall, is much more recent (1913) than the rest of the building and, as is often noted, gives the impression of nothing so much as a more-important-than-usual branch of Barclays Bank. To get a better (and more sympathetic) feeling of what lies behind the façade, walk down Buckingham Gate, and appreciate the side view of the palace. The Queen's private quarters are on the other side, overlooking Constitution Hill. (There is a charge for the summer tours of the interior of the palace, as there is for admission to the Queen's Gallery or the Royal Mews.) One of the most opportune times to visit, of course, is for the Changing of the Guard (see also). / www.royal.gov.uk; Tube: St James's Park, Victoria, Green Park.

Cleopatra's Needle WC2
Victoria Embankment   2–2D
This 3,500-year-old obelisk, weighing about 186 tons, now by the side of the Thames, was taken from near the Temple of the Sun God in Heliopolis in Egypt. It was presented to Britain by the Turkish Viceroy in 1819 and has a twin, which stands in New York's Central Park. The two lions which 'guard' the needle were incorrectly placed (they should actually face away, to be able to keep watch), but their position has never been corrected. / Tube: Embankment.

Coram's Fields WC1
93 Guilford St   (020) 7837 6138   2–1D
Seven acres of central London to which adults (over 16) are not admitted – unless accompanied by a child! This shady playground – the legacy of an c18 philanthropist – is a boon for harassed parents. It boasts play equipment, a sports area, paddling pool, pets corner and a duck pond. Note: the house in which Charles Dickens lived is quite close, at 48 Doughty Street. / Times: 9am-8pm (Easter to end Oct), dusk (Winter); Tube: Russell Square; café school holidays only.

Covent Garden WC2
(020) 7836 9136   2–2C
Covent Garden, with its c18 market setting and its colourful shops, stalls and cafés, is one of the most agreeable and popular places for a stroll in central London. There's almost invariably something going on in the way of musical performances, busking or more serious street-theatre – the Market office (on the number given) can provide information about forthcoming attractions. The highlight is the May Fayre (see Events). Of particular interest is the newly-refurbished Royal Opera House on the east side of Covent Garden. The building's gleaming Floral Hall is now an open public space. Just north of Covent Garden lies Neal Street. This was formerly a warehouse district, but now is refurbished, with eccentric stores, restaurants and regular street performers. / www.coventgardenmarket.co.uk; Tube: Covent Garden, Leicester Square; café.

Eros SW1
Piccadilly Circus   2–2C
Although invariably known as Eros, the famous, small statue at Piccadilly Circus in fact represents the Angel of Christian Charity. Unveiled in 1893, it was London's first statue to be made of aluminium, at the time a rare and unusual material. It commemorates the philanthropist Lord Shaftesbury, whose Avenue is nearby. / Tube: Piccadilly Circus.

Fortnum & Mason Clock W1
181 Piccadilly   2–2B
On the hour, every hour, four-foot-high figures of Mr Fortnum and Mr Mason emerge from doors above the shop's main entrance, face each other and bow. A c18 air is then played on 17 bells. The two gentlemen then bow again and retire to their respective quarters. All-in-all, it's quite an amusing performance from one of London's few performing clocks. (See also Swiss Centre.) / www.fortnumandmason.com; Tube: Piccadilly Circus, Green Park.

Green Park SW1
(020) 7930 1793   2–3B
The park was originally meadowland used for hunting, and duels were regularly fought here until the mid-c17. Now the 53 acres by Piccadilly comprise what the unkind might describe as the Ugly Duckling of the Royal Parks – alone among them, it lacks a lake, flowers, summer music and café. It is, however, a relaxing place and very central. Constitution Hill (which runs along the park's southern border) is so-called in commemoration of Charles II's morning walks. / Times: 24 hours; www.royalparks.co.uk; Tube: Green Park, Hyde Park Corner.

Old Bond Street W1
2–2B
If you're seriously into window-shopping, you certainly shouldn't miss the extraordinary row of shops to be found in this street which, for more than three centuries, has been one of London's most fashionable boutique thoroughfares – and which is currently enjoying a new wave of popularity. All the shops whose very names conjure up visions of opulence are there – Cartier, Tiffany, Versace, to name but three. Extravagantly-scaled boutiques of recent opening include Donna Karan, Prada and Ralph Lauren. Most of the best names are in Old Bond Street, but, externally at least, the most impressive shop of all is Asprey/Garrard (jewellers and goldsmiths) of 165 New Bond Street. / Tube: Green Park.

Riverside Walk
See the introduction of the South section for suggestions of interesting walks by the Thames.

Roman Bath* WC2
5 Strand Ln   2–2D
A whodunnit (or rather 'who built it') mystery surrounds the remains of a bath restored in the c17 and believed by some people to be Roman. It's owned by the National Trust and there is an entry fee, but if you find your way down the steps and into the narrow lane off the Strand, 90 per cent of what there is to see is visible through the window. Peer in, read the printed notice and decide the origins for yourself. / Times: 24 hours (light switch operational from outside); Tube: Temple (not Sun), Blackfriars, Charing Cross.

St James's Park SW1
(020) 7930 1793   2–3C
This is possibly the most beautiful, and certainly the most highly cultivated, of the Royal Parks. Situated as it is, in the ceremonial heart of London, between Westminster and Buckingham Palace, it offers idyllic views in both directions. The park (93 acres in extent) was acquired by Henry VIII as a deer park for St James's Palace, but owes much of its current appearance to John Nash, whose designs were commissioned in the reign of George IV. During the summer, there are frequent weekend concerts at the bandstand and gun salutes (see also) on ceremonial occasions. The pelicans are fed at 3pm every afternoon, by Duck Island. / Times: 24 hours; www.royalparks.co.uk; Tube: St James's Park; café.

Speaker's Corner W2
Hyde Park (NE corner)   2–2A
For more than a century, this has been the London home of the soapbox orator – Sunday sees the expression of a kaleidoscope of views, from the slightly off-beat to the decidedly cranky. The 'official' website given lists famous people who have voiced their opinions in the past, and demonstrations which have begun here (including meetings of the Suffragette movement). / Times: Sun afternoon; www.speakerscorner.net; Tube: Marble Arch.

Swiss Centre Clock W1
Leicester Sq   2–2C
The Swiss Centre boasts a fine 27-bell glockenspiel, which plays Brahms, classical Swiss folk tunes and folk music from around the world. It was built in 1985 and dedicated to the City of Westminster to celebrate its 400th anniversary. Sounding the hour takes about five minutes, during which an Alpine procession of cows, sheep, milkmaids, etc makes its way around the base of the clock. There are performances at noon, 6pm, 7pm and 8pm every day, and, at weekends and bank holidays, on the hour every hour, between noon and 8pm, except 1pm. / Tube: Piccadilly Circus, Leicester Square.

Trafalgar Square WC2
2–2C
This great, central square, dominated by the National Gallery (see also) is famous for its 170-foot high column dedicated to the memory of Lord Nelson (1843), its fountains and, despite Mr Mayor's best efforts, its pigeons. The statues of imperial lions (Landseer, 1867) are also well known, despite the fact that real lions never sit as represented – they always lie on their side. Plans are currently afoot to pedestrianise the north road of the square, connecting the island to the steps of the National Gallery (see also). / Tube: Leicester Square, Charing Cross.

Victoria Embankment Gardens WC2

Villiers St   Festival details:
Alternative Arts (020) 7375 0441   2–2D
This colourful, elongated park lies a few short steps from the traffic and bustle of the Strand. Spring and summer usher in not only a profusion of blooms but also an array of entertainments, such as dance, mime, music, poetry and opera festivals. In spite of its attraction and especially considering the major road running alongside, it is surprisingly peaceful. An ideal spot to lunch – nearby Villiers Street has a plethora of sandwich shops – it's very popular with local office workers at lunchtimes. York Watergate (1626) is an attractive curiosity, and there are many plaques and explanatory notices about the history of the area to educate you. The largest of these reminds you that, until the construction of the Embankment in 1828, all of what is today a garden was submerged beneath the Thames!
/ Tube: Charing Cross, Embankment; café.

Victoria Tower Gardens SW1

Millbank   2–4D
This quiet and extremely scenic garden, beneath the looming presence of the Victoria Tower (at the other end of the Houses of Parliament from Big Ben) is graced by a cast of Rodin's Six Burghers of Calais and a bronze of the Suffragette, Emmeline Pankhurst, as well as a children's play area. / Times: 7am–dusk; Tube: Westminster.

Wellington Arch* W1

Hyde Park Corner   (020) 8995 0508   2–3A
The Wellington Arch bears the largest piece of sculpture in London, Quadriga, by Adrian Jones (1912), in which a figure of Peace descends upon the Chariot of War. The neo-classical Arch itself was built to celebrate the Duke of Wellington's victories over Napoleon, and was completed in 1828, originally bearing a gigantic statue of the Iron Duke himself. Before restoration by English Heritage in 1997, the arch contained London's smallest police station. Colourful new illuminations make night-time visits the most rewarding, and a museum has been opened, for which there is a charge. / Times: museum 10am–6pm, Wed–Sun; Tube: Hyde Park Corner.

West London

Introduction

West London offers a lot of possibilities to those who want to combine a little artistic or intellectual interest (perhaps a trip to the **Victoria & Albert Museum** or the **Serpentine Gallery**) with a visit to one of the beautiful parks which dot the area, such as **Hyde Park**, **Kensington Gardens** or **Holland Park**.

This combination makes it an excellent area for days out with children, for whom the **Natural History** and **Science Museums** are top attractions. Both those museums are open free of charge only later in the day, so it makes sense to do a park first, and to finish on an educational note.

Away from the centre and its famous parks, the area is rich with fine houses and gardens, such as **Osterley Park** and **Chiswick House**. Take a picnic, and both places should, if the weather is fine, provide a good day out. Both houses are convenient for a riverside walk, either for a stroll after lunch or for some more serious exercise. For those who prefer to amble in a more urban environment, the pleasures of Saturday's **Portobello Road market** are hard to beat.

Some lesser-known central attractions well worth investigating include the **Royal Hospital** (and the neighbouring **Ranelagh Gardens**) in Chelsea and **Leighton House Museum and Art Gallery** in Holland Park. Further out, **Pitshanger Manor Museum** and **Gunnersbury Park Museum** offer interesting and attractive houses to visit, set in pleasant parks.

Suggested walk

A casual walk in this section of London can lead you through elegant shopping and fine contemporary art. Begin at Sloane Square and head north along Sloane Street with its impressive fashion shops. Turn left up Pont Street to Beauchamp Place, famous for its chi-chi shops and 'village' atmosphere. Keep going and you're on Brompton Road – turn right and quickly the massive shopping icon of Harrods looms.

Continue east along the Brompton Road, perhaps, stopping to admire the designer collections at Harvey Nichols and its impressive top-floor food hall. At the end of Brompton Road, cross Knightsbridge to enter Hyde Park – an ideal spot for a picnic. In the park, stroll along the Serpentine, perhaps, checking out the latest contemporary art show at the Serpentine Gallery.

Chelsea Information Office SW3

Old Town Hall, King's Rd   (020) 7352 6056   3–3C
*Chelsea's information office is in the same building as a
good reference library; the hours are the same for both.*
/ Times: Mon-Sat 10am-8pm (Wed 1pm, Fri & Sat 5pm); Tube: Sloane Square,
South Kensington.

Hillingdon Tourist Information Centre, Middx

Uxbridge Central Library, High St, Uxbridge
(01895) 250706
The TIC and library keep the same hours. / Times: Mon-Fri
9.30am-8pm (Wed & Fri 5.30pm, Sat 4pm); www.hillingdon.gov.uk;
Tube: Uxbridge.

Hounslow Tourist Information Centre, Middx

Treaty Centre, High St, Hounslow   (020) 8583 2929
*The TIC has information on the local May Day festival and the
Chiswick Extravaganza at Chiswick House, usually occurring on
the August bank holiday weekend.* / Times: Mon-Sat 9.30am-5.30pm
(Tue & Thu 8pm); Tube: Hounslow Central.

Twickenham Tourist Information Centre, Middx

Civic Centre, 44 York St   (020) 8891 7272
/ Times: Mon-Fri 9am-5.15pm (5pm Fri); BR: Twickenham.

Indoor attractions

Baden-Powell House SW7

Queen's Gate   (020) 7584 7031   3–2B
*After the death of Baden-Powell in 1941, Boy Scouts around
the world raised money for a 'living memorial'. The result was
this hostel, opened, in 1961. There is a small display about the
life of Baden-Powell and the Scout Movement in the reception
area. (The archives of the movement – dating back to 1907 –
have been moved to a location in Essex; call (020) 8524 5246
for an appointment to view them.)* / Times: 24 hours;
www.scoutbase.org.uk; Tube: South Kensington, Gloucester Road; café.

Boston Manor House, Middx

Boston Manor Rd, Brentford   (020) 8560 5441
*This Jacobean manor was built in 1623 and extended in 1670,
when it was bought by the Clitherow family, whose home it
remained until 1924. The first floor State Rooms have English
Renaissance plaster ceilings and impressive historic furniture.
The drawing room ceiling of 1623 has panels representing the
five senses, the four elements, War & Peace, Peace & Plenty,
and Faith, Hope & Charity. The early c19 ground floor rooms
house paintings relating to the locality.* / Times: Sat, Sun & bank hols
2.30pm-5pm, from 1st Sat in Apr to last Sun in Oct;
www.cip.org.uk/heritage/boston.htm; Tube: Boston Manor.

Czech Memorial Scrolls Centre SW7

Westminster Synagogue, Kent House, Rutland Gardens
(020) 7581 8012   3–1C

In 1963, 1,564 Torah scrolls were acquired from communist Prague – part of the vast collection of Jewish ritual items confiscated by Hitler, who planned to exhibit them in a 'museum of an extinct race'. This exhibition tells their story, something of the history of the communities they came from, the retrieval of the scrolls by the trust and their subsequent restoration and dispersal to Jewish communities around the world. Beautifully decorated bibles and wimpels are also on display. / Times: Tue & Thu 10am-4pm; www.czechtorah.org/trust.htm; Tube: Knightsbridge.

Goethe Institute SW7

50 Princes Gate, Exhibition Rd   (020) 7596 4000   3–1C

The Institute, the German cultural centre, has a small gallery which has changing exhibitions of works in some way connected with the country. Small parties (one or two people) can pre-book to view a video from the extensive collection, which includes documentaries and dramas. In early 2001, the gallery re-opened after an extensive refurbishment. The Institute's task is "to promote the German language and to foster international cultural co-operation", to which end it organises various events on German culture. / Times: Mon-Thu 12pm-8pm, Sat 11am-5pm; www.goethe.de/london; Tube: South Kensington; café.

Gunnersbury Park Museum W3

Gunnersbury Park, Popes Ln   (020) 8992 1612   1–3A

This very grand local museum recently celebrated 75 years of opening to the public. It houses a large collection on the history of Ealing and Hounslow, but also temporary exhibitions on wider themes – not always of purely local interest – and there are occasional talks relating to the collections. Housed in a former Rothschild family house, built in 1835 on the site of a former royal residence, it benefits from an extremely pleasant park location. On summer weekends you can visit the original Victorian kitchens. / Times: Apr-Oct 1pm-5pm (Sat, Sun & bank hols 6pm), Nov-Mar 1pm-4pm; kitchens (summer only) 1pm-4pm; www.cip.org.uk/parks/gp/museum.htm; Tube: Acton Town; café (summer only).

Heathrow Airport, Middx

Newall Rd   Visitors Centre (020) 8745 6655,
Roof Garden recorded info line (020) 8745 5259

Heathrow is staggering in the scale of its operations, handling more than 60 million passengers a year (and more international passengers than any other airport in the world). There is a Visitors Centre, which houses a viewing gallery and an exhibition with interactive technology concerning the airport's past, present and future. Worksheets are available for children. There is also a roof garden between Terminals 1 & 2 (9am-dusk daily). From the viewing area in the Queen's Building, you can watch all the comings and goings of the aeroplanes. / Times: 10am-5pm daily; www.baa.co.uk; Tube: Heathrow Terminals.

Hillingdon Local Heritage Service, Middx

Uxbridge Central Library, High St, Uxbridge
(01895) 250702

*The borough doesn't have a dedicated museum but makes
do with a small display space in the Central Library. Here you
find changing exhibitions and a local studies room. There are
periodic events and free internet access for the public.*
/ Times: main library, Mon-Thu 9.30am-8pm (Wed 5.30pm), Fri
10am-5.30pm, Sat 9.30am-4pm; local studies library Mon 9.30am-8pm,
Tue-Thu 1am-5.30pm, Fri 10am-5.30pm, Sat 9.30am-12pm & 1am-4pm;
www.hillingdon.gov.uk; Tube: Uxbridge.

Hogarth's House W4

Hogarth Lane, Great West Rd   (020) 8994 6757   1–3A

*The Chiswick home of the great English engraver and painter
William Hogarth (1697-1764) was restored in 1997 to
celebrate the tercentenary of his birth. It contains memorabilia
of his life, work and circle. The main attractions, however, are
his most famous series of engravings (such as Marriage à la
Mode and the Rake's Progress) and the attractive garden,
which contains a mulberry tree dating from the painter's time.*
/ Times: Tue-Sun 1pm-4pm (Sat & Sun 6pm), (Nov-Mar 5pm); closed January;
Tube: Turnham Green.

Leighton House Museum & Art Gallery W14

12 Holland Park Rd   (020) 7602 3316   1–3B

*No visitor to Holland Park should miss this extraordinary mid-
Victorian house, with later Moorish Hall (complete with small
pool). It is a wonderful setting for the permanent collection
of paintings by Frederic, Lord Leighton (1830–96) and some
of his contemporaries. In summer, the garden, which contains
some sculptures, is open. There are also temporary exhibitions
in the recently refurbished Perrin Gallery – if you want to
assess current standards in what was once London's most
famous artistic quarter, don't miss the Kensington and Chelsea
Artists' Show in July.* / Times: Wed-Mon 11am-5.30pm;
www.aboutbritain.com/LeightonHouseArtGallery.htm; Tube: Kensington High
Street.

Lindsey House SW10

99-100 Cheyne Walk
(01494) 528051 (National Trust)   3–3C

*Overlooking the Thames, this building dates from 1674 and
is on the site of Sir Thomas More's garden. Despite being
owned by the National Trust, it is tenanted, so sightseeing
is by appointment only (via the Trust's regional office on the
number given) and only on four selected dates per year. Visits
are restricted to the ground floor entrance hall, main staircase,
first floors and gardens, but you can admire the splendid c17
exterior at any time.* / Times: by appt in writing to Mr Bourne, 100
Cheyne Walk, London SW10 0DQ (include SAE); Tube: Sloane Square or
South Kensington (both around 1.5 miles away).

Martinware Pottery Collection, Middx
Southall Library, Osterley Park Road, Southall
(020) 8574 3412
*Martinware Pottery was made by the Martin brothers at their
factory in Southall between 1877 & 1923. Their output is a
good example of Victorian art pottery – the brothers were best
known for their bird sculptures and bowls, vessels adorned with
sea creatures, and tiles, designed in a capricious but highly
skilled style.* / Times: Tue-Sat 9.30am-7.45pm (Fri & Sat 5pm); BR: Southall.

Narwhal Inuit Art Gallery W4
55 Linden Gardens   (020) 8747 1575   1–3A
*A gallery with an unusual theme – Inuit (Eskimo) art of
Canada, Russia, Alaska and Greenland. The culture dates back
15,000 years, and, even though there is no Inuit word for 'art',
the collection includes sculptures, prints, wallhangings,
ceramics, woven baskets, embroidery, carvings and graphics.
View by prior appointment only.* / www.niaef.com; Tube: Turnham
Green.

National Army Museum SW3
Royal Hospital Rd   (020) 7730 0717   3–3D
*The Army's own museum relates its history, from the archers
of Henry V to involvement in contemporary UN peacekeeping
operations. The emphasis is on the story of the individual
soldier – the "human aspect". There is a major collection of
uniforms, life-sized models in costumes through the ages,
paintings of famous battle scenes, portraits by Reynolds and
Gainsborough and displays of weaponry and medals, as well
as some interactive aspects – visitors are welcome to try on
helmets and play with the dioramas. A visit here makes a good
fit with a trip to the neighbouring Royal Hospital (see also).*
/ Times: 10am-5.30pm; www.national-army-museum.ac.uk;
Tube: Sloane Square.

Natural History Museum* SW7
Cromwell Rd   (020) 7938 9123   3–2C
*Free time is short at this famous museum – at weekends
you get only 50 minutes, so may we suggest a few of the
key attractions. You will want to spend a few minutes in
the cathedral-like central hall, before taking in the Dinosaurs
exhibition – the newest addition to the dinosaur pit is the
fearsome, robotic, Tyrannosaurus Rex who not only moves
and roars, but also smells realistic! You might also like to find
out how your body works, by visiting the Human Biology
Gallery. The museum has many interactive displays – it even
offers the possibility of 'experiencing' the Kobe earthquake
(as felt inside a supermarket) that created havoc in Japan –
and is most definitely worth a return visit or two.* / Times: Mon-Fri
4.30pm-5.50pm; Sat, Sun & bank hols 5pm-5.50pm; www.nhm.ac.uk;
Tube: South Kensington.

The Orangery & the Ice House W8

Holland Park   (020) 7603 1123   3–1A

The charming c18 glasshouse in the centre of Holland Park and the nearby Ice House are used for five high-quality arts and crafts exhibitions in various media per year. Call for further information on exhibitions and hours in operation.
/ Times: 11am-7pm (during exhibitions); Tube: Kensington High Street, Holland Park; café.

Orleans House Gallery, Middx

Riverside, Twickenham   (020) 8892 0221

Twickenham benefits from an unusually attractive gallery in which to display its borough art collection and to hold contemporary art exhibitions (around five per year). It was designed by James Gibbs in 1720, as the garden pavilion of a very grand house (itself demolished two centuries later) and is richly decorated with ornamental mouldings and gilt. The setting, in a picturesque woodland garden by the Thames (open daylight hours), is a good place for a picnic or as a starting point for a stroll along the river. During the summer (Apr-Oct), one can also visit the Stables Gallery, which holds frequently changing exhibitions. / Times: Tue-Sat 1pm-5.30pm (Oct-Mar 4.30pm), Sun & bank hols 2pm-5.30pm (Oct-Mar 4.30pm); www.richmond.gov.uk; Tube: Richmond or BR: St Margarets (closer than tube).

Pitshanger Manor Museum W5

Mattock Ln   (020) 8567 1227   1–3A

This Ealing house, set in a park, already had the benefit of some exquisite plaster work designed by George Dance in the mid-c18, when it attracted the attentions of the great neo-classical architect, Sir John Soane. Between 1800 and 1810, he transformed the house into a Regency villa for himself and his family. The building (Grade I listed, and open to the public since 1987) merits a visit in its own right. There is also a changing display of Martinware – the pottery made by the Martin brothers of Southall between 1877 and 1923 – and an art gallery with changing exhibitions of contemporary art.
/ Times: Tue-Sat 10am-5pm; Tube: Ealing Broadway; café.

Polish Institute & Sikorsi Museum SW7

20 Princes Gate   (020) 7589 9249   3–1C

Anyone with even a passing interest in Poland or in military history should visit this elegant museum near Hyde Park – it is by far the most important collection of Polish material anywhere outside that country. There are important momentoes of the many conflicts in which Poles have been involved – including the national flag flown over the ruins of the monastery of Monte Cassino in 1944. The archives contain around two million documents as well as other materials from the Polish Government and Polish Embassies around the world, mostly from WWII (when they came to London rather than to the Communist Government in Poland). A photograph and film archive is also available for viewing. / Times: Mon-Fri 2pm-4pm; 1st Sat of month 10am-4pm; archives Tue-Fri 9.30am-4pm; Tube: South Kensington, Knightsbridge.

Royal College of Art SW7
Kensington Gore   (020) 7590 4444   3–1B

This is the only exclusively post-graduate university of art and design in the world – famous graduates include David Hockney, Henry Moore and Barbara Hepworth. Courses range from painting, through fashion, to vehicle design and curating. There's almost always an exhibition in progress and most are free – but call the Public Relations office on (020) 7590 4121 before you set out to avoid disappointment. / Times: during exhibitions, Mon-Fri 10am-6pm; www.rca.ac.uk; Tube: Knightsbridge, South Kensington, Kensington High Street.

Royal College of Music – Department of Portraits & Performance History SW7
Prince Consort Rd   (020) 7591 4340   3–1B

The collections house displays portraits and busts – of musicians, of course – mainly from the c19 and early c20. Designs for instruments and concert halls, and a performance history archive of over 600,000 programmes are also to be found here. In addition, there are hundreds of original watercolours, engravings and photographs catalogued but not on display (call for an appointment to view them). Note: the collection is housed in a sixth floor gallery, to which there is no lift. / Times: Mon-Fri 10am-5.30pm by telephone appt; www.rcm.ac.uk; Tube: South Kensington, Gloucester Road.

Royal Hospital SW3
Royal Hospital Rd   (020) 7730 5282   3–3D

Wren's elegant 1682 building, founded by Charles II for veteran soldiers, is still the home of the Chelsea Pensioners, who can sometimes be spotted around the area wearing their splendid scarlet uniforms. Indeed, give two weeks notice and a tour, guided by one of the pensioners, can be arranged. The Great Hall, the Chapel and the Museum may be visited. Don't miss the lovely grounds, Ranelagh Gardens (see also). / Times: Mon-Sat 10am-12pm & 2pm-4pm; www.chelseapensioner.org.uk; Tube: Sloane Square.

Royal Military School of Music, Middx
Kneller Hall, Kneller Rd, Twickenham   (020) 8898 5533

This collection of instruments used by the military includes wind and stringed items from the past three centuries. Of particular interest perhaps is a bugle played at the Battle of Waterloo and indigenous percussion instruments including 'talking drums' from Africa. Tours can include a visit to the Chapel and the museum, and hearing a band in rehearsal. / Times: by written appt, generally Wed mornings Jun-Aug; www.army.mod.uk/ceremonialandheritage/museums/details/m148scho.htm; BR: Whitton; café.

Science Museum* SW7
Exhibition Rd   (08708) 704771   3–1C

Appropriately for the prime technological museum of the first industrial nation, the 200,000 exhibits contain many 'firsts' – the first steam engine of the c18 and the first steam turbine of the c19, Stephenson's train (the Rocket) and the Vickers Vimy aircraft which made the first non-stop Atlantic crossing in 1919. Many attractions are more contemporary, including the Apollo 10 spacecraft, still scorched from re-entry into the atmosphere. There's always a great deal going on throughout the museum, and there are enough 'hands-on' exhibits in the 40 galleries to keep children from as young as three happy. Six new interactive galleries, ranging from digital technology to genetics, were recently added. There are charges for some special exhibitions. / Times: 4.30pm-6pm; www.sciencemuseum.org.uk; Tube: South Kensington; café.

Serpentine Gallery W2
Kensington Gardens   (020) 7298 1515 info line   3–1C

The attractive and popular Hyde Park gallery re-opened in February 1998 after a major renovation. It stages a number of modern and contemporary exhibitions of artists from around the globe. There are usually talks by artists and critics on Saturday afternoons at 3pm. / Times: 10am-6pm; www.serpentinegallery.org; Tube: Lancaster Gate, South Kensington; café.

Victoria & Albert Museum* SW7
Cromwell Rd   (020) 7938 8500, (020) 7938 8349   3–2C

Founded in 1852, the "world's largest decorative arts and design museum" comprises 145 galleries, reflecting centuries of artistic achievement from Europe, the Far East, South East Asia and the Islamic world. There are extensive collections of ceramics, furniture, jewellery and dress, from ancient times to the present day. A star attraction is a collection of Raphael's seven tapestry cartoons – preparatory designs for tapestries – depicting the acts of Christ's apostles. The cartoons, claimed among the greatest artistic treasures in Britain, were originally commissioned by Pope Leo XI for the Sistine Chapel.

From November 2001, the British Galleries will be re-displayed as fifteen new galleries telling the story of British design and decorative art from 1500-1900. The galleries will include 3,000 exhibits, enhanced by interactive computers, video screens and audio programmes. The English silver galleries are a noteworthy display of over 1,200 objects, dating from 1300–1800. The museum, once free to all, now as a general rule only charges working adults. However, there is free access after 4.30pm and once you are in – unusually for London's larger collections – there are no additional charges for any exhibition. / Times: Mon-Sun 4.30pm-5.45pm (Wed 10pm); www.vam.ac.uk; Tube: South Kensington.

William Morris Society W6

Kelmscott House, 26 Upper Mall   (020) 8741 3735   1–3A
*Occupying part of the house in which Morris – socialist,
designer and author – lived from 1878 until his death in 1896,
this small collection of memorabilia, designs and books includes
one of the original presses on which his novels, poetry and
pamphlets were printed. (Devotees should also see the entry
for the William Morris Gallery in the East End section.)*
/ Times: Thu & Sat 2pm-5pm; www.ccny.cuny.edu/wmorris;
Tube: Ravenscourt Park.

Outdoor attractions

Albert Memorial SW7

Prince's Gate, Kensington Gore   3–1B
*The Albert Memorial – for many years shrouded in scaffolding
– can now be seen in all its opulent splendour. The memorial
was conceived in 1852, to celebrate the Great Exhibition (the
Crystal Palace having just been dismantled and removed from
Hyde Park), and was to feature a statue of Victoria's consort,
Prince Albert. However, his death in 1861 (years before
completion of the monument) changed the focus completely.
It is decorated with nearly 200 statues representing the arts,
sciences, industries, continents and moral virtues, while the
frieze of Parnassus depicts 169 life-size figures of the world's
artistic geniuses. (Interestingly, the Prince hated the idea
that his statue should be placed in the memorial – "it would
disturb my quiet rides in Rotten Row to see my own face
staring at me.")* / Tube: Knightsbridge, South Kensington.

Brent Lodge Park W7

Church Rd, Hanwell   (020) 8566 1929   1–2A
*Once known as 'the bunny park' because of its teeming rabbit
population, this expansive area – some 800 acres – has wide
open spaces surrounded by dense pockets of trees, and makes
a good destination for a quiet picnic or a family day out. The
river Brent crosses directly through the park, and there are a
number of small bridges connecting the two sections. There is
an animal centre (part of which has an entry charge) housing
guinea pigs, rabbits and pheasants, to name a few of the furry
creatures you might encounter there.* / Times: 7am-dusk;
www.ealing.gov.uk/Parks; BR: Hanwell or 207 bus or E1 or E3 buses; café.

Burnham Beeches, Bucks

Farnham Common   (01753) 647358
*Though not quite IN London, this famous beauty spot – one
of the finest examples of ancient woodland in Britain – can
fairly claim to be OF the capital city as it has been owned by
the Corporation of London for more than a century. The most
famous feature of the 540-acre site is the beech pollards,
some of which are almost 500 years old.*

There is a programme of regular free walks and talks, and usually an annual open day in late June (call for details). The latter offers a chance to see displays of falconry, countryside management techniques and examples of country crafts. Given the wood's accessibility (just north of Junction 6 of the M4), it would be the perfect place to get away from it all if it were not for the fact that every year half a million other people have the same idea! Autumn is the very best time to visit. / Times: pedestrians 24 hours; vehicles 8am-one hour after sunset; www.cityoflondon.gov.uk; BR: Slough (then bus to Farnham Common).

Bushy Park, Middx
(020) 8979 1586
This ancient deer park was part of Wren's grand design for neighbouring Hampton Court. Herds of red and fallow deer roam its 1,100 acres. The Woodland Gardens, with their fine azaleas, camellias and rhododendrons, are a post-war addition and make a nice place for a picnic. They boast a fine chestnut avenue which is the focal point of Chestnut Sunday, a traditional Victorian parade and picnic, which takes place on the second Sunday in May and celebrates the blossoming of the trees. / Times: 6.30am-dusk summer (7pm winter); www.royalparks.co.uk; BR: Hampton Wick.

Chelsea Harbour SW10
(020) 7225 9100   3–4B
This contemporary riverside development never seems to have lived up to its aspirations, but it is an attractive marina and it makes a pleasant place for a riverside walk – despite its relatively central location, the Harbour has a surprisingly far-away feel. Reflecting the proximity of many of London's grander residential areas, the development has become a centre for interior design firms. They are strictly 'trade only', but there is an annual open day in March, highlighting new trends in interior design. / Tube: Earl's Court (then C3 bus).

Chiswick House* W4
Burlington Ln   (020) 8995 5390   1–3A
The mainly wooded, 64-acre gardens of this fine neo-classical villa have suitably Italianate highlights – statues, temples, urns and obelisks – and there is also a lake and a cascade waterfall. The information centre, currently in a Portakabin, has a small exhibition about the history of the garden and can equip you with a park trails pamphlet and map. There is a picnic area (and also a café). The house (to which there is an entry charge) is run by English Heritage. / Times: park 8am-dusk (approx 5.15pm in winter, 9.30pm in summer); information centre 9am-30 minutes before the park closes; Tube: Turnham Green (then E3 bus); café.

Crane Park Island, Middx

Crane Park, Twickenham   (020) 7261 0447

This small island (just over four acres), accessed by bridge, has its place in history – the old gunpowder mill here (now demolished) is believed to have been where Guy Fawkes obtained his supplies. Nowadays, its attractions are more peaceful, and it's an agreeable site, run by the London Wildlife Trust. Due to the cleanliness of its water, it is home to the rare water vole, and also safe for kids to paddle in. There are also three paths, one of which (the Hobbin Path) is suitable for disabled people. During the summer holidays, there is a playscheme – call for details. The Shot Tower is being converted into a visitors centre with information on the history of the site and the wildlife in it. It is due to be completed in 2001, and a viewing platform at the top is envisaged. / Times: 24 hours; www.wildlifetrust.org.uk/london/reserves; BR: Whitton.

Garrick's Temple & Lawn at Hampton

Hampton Court Rd
(020) 8892 0221 (Orleans House Gallery)
or (020) 8255 4903 (Hampton Riverside Trust)

This garden building on the Thames, a 10 minute walk from Hampton Court Palace, was built in 1755-6 by David Garrick, England's second most famous actor, dramatist and theatre manager, to commemorate his idol, William Shakespeare. After a recent restoration, the opportunity was taken to install a display traversing Garrick's acting career and his Hampton private life. / Times: Temple: April-Sept. Sundays 2pm-5pm and by appt.; Lawn: Daily throughout the year 7.30am-dusk; BR: Hampton Court and then R68 bus or Hampton and then 111 or 216 bus.

Gunnersbury Triangle Nature Reserve W4

Bollo Ln   (020) 8747 3881   1–3A

This six-acre site developed a rich covering of vegetation after being surrounded by railway tracks in the late c19. Since then it has been undisturbed, apart from some allotments, until it was threatened by development in the early '80s and became a 'test case'. The conservationists won, and this was the first time that a planning inspector had preferred nature conservation to development on a city site. It is now managed by the local volunteers of the London Wildlife Trust and during summer school holidays there is a usually a full-time warden (daily) and a programme of free events. / Times: Tue 10am-4pm, Fri & Sun 2pm-4.30pm; also some Sats & school hols; www.chiswickw4.com; Tube: Chiswick Park.

Hampton Court Palace*, Middx
(020) 8781 9500
The wonderful gardens and park of Wolsey's great riverside palace (completed by Henry VIII and substantially altered by William and Mary) are open to the public without charge. The formal gardens are the most visited free attraction of their type in the country. They include features from Victorian times, as well as from the earlier periods of the palace's construction, and a riverside walk. Around the gardens, in the 560-acre area that includes both Bushey and Home parks, graze the descendants of the deer hunted by Tudor monarchs. There is a charge for access to the Palace itself. / Times: 8am-dusk; www.hrp.org.uk; BR: Hampton Court; café.

Holland Park W8
Ilchester Place   (020) 7602 9483   1–3B
Until some forty years ago, Holland Park was an extraordinary hangover from former days – a private 'country' estate, in the middle of London. It maintains a unique and charming character, and, in spite of its relatively small size (52 acres), some of it is heavily wooded (and managed so as to enhance wildlife). Apart from its superb formal gardens, it benefits from the Kyoto Garden, installed by Japanese benefactors in 1991. Visit just before sunset to witness the peacocks' bedtime, when the birds fly into the trees and screech to one another. Other attractions include a large adventure playground and the Ecology Centre, which has a series of free talks. There are also educational events for organised groups (details from the Ecology Service) including pond dipping for children, and a conservation programme for volunteers of all ages. The Park contains the Orangery and the Ice House (see also). / Times: 7.30am-30 mins before dusk; www.rbkc.gov.uk; Tube: Holland Park, Kensington High Street.

Hyde Park W2
(020) 7298 2000   3–1C
The greatest of the central Royal Parks was originally acquired by Henry VIII from the Abbey at Westminster as a private hunting ground. In 1637, when Charles I opened it to the public, it became notorious as a haunt of footpads and thieves. (William III later had 300 oil lamps erected to deter them, creating Britain's first artificially-lit highway.) The giant glass structure of Crystal Palace covered almost eight hectares of the park when it was erected for the Great Exhibition of 1851.

The park's 344 acres now offer a variety of attractions, ranging from the formal gardens along its south side, Rotten Row (a bridleway for more than 300 years, its name derived from the French 'Route du Roi'), a river (the Serpentine) and areas of woods and grass. There is a children's playground and a Pet Cemetery (open only one day a year in Sept; look for posters around the park advertising the date). In summer, there are weekend and bank holiday concerts at the bandstand (afternoons and evenings). Speakers' Corner (see also) is situated in the north east corner of the park. Kensington Gardens (see also) adjoin the park, and many more attractions can be found there. / Times: 5am-12am; www.royalparks.co.uk; Tube: Knightsbridge, Hyde Park Corner, Marble Arch, Lancaster Gate, Queensway.

Kensington Gardens W2
(020) 7298 2117   3–1B
These were the private gardens of Kensington Palace (designed by Wren) and were largely laid out under the direction of Queen Caroline in 1728. The gardens were opened to the public by Queen Victoria and are effectively an extension of Hyde Park (see also). Attractions in the 275 acres include the Round Pond for boating (model boats only, please) where the Model Boat Club meets every Sunday morning, the charming small statue of Peter Pan and the very pretty area in the immediate vicinity of the Palace itself. The gardens also house the Serpentine Gallery and the Albert Memorial (see also). In 2000, the Diana Memorial Playground replaced one of the original playgrounds. It is based on a Peter Pan theme and is open 10am-dusk. In summer, there are weekly concerts at the bandstand, occasional country dancing displays and children's entertainments. / Times: dawn-dusk; www.royalparks.co.uk; Tube: Bayswater, Lancaster Gate, Queensway, Kensington High Street; café.

Kensington Roof Gardens W8
Barkers Department Store, Kensington High St (enter from 99 Derry St)   (020) 7937 7994   3–1A
Opened in the 1930s, this extraordinary 6th-floor installation is Europe's largest roof garden, and is most certainly worth a visit. It is now home to a nightclub owned by Sir Richard Branson, but (subject to prior club commitments) daytime visitors are welcome. There are in fact three adjoining gardens – an English woodland garden with flamingos, a Tudor garden and a Spanish garden with palm trees. / Times: 10am-5pm, but call first; www.roofgardens.com; Tube: Kensington High Street.

Marble Hill House*, Middx
Richmond Rd, Twickenham   (020) 8892 5115
Built in the 1720s as a retreat from court life for Henrietta Howard, Countess of Suffolk (George II's mistress), this Palladian villa – one of the most perfect surviving examples of the type – inhabits a large park which stretches down to the river. There is an admission charge for the house, but access to the grounds is free. / Times: dawn-dusk; www.guidetorichmond.co.uk; Tube: Richmond; café.

Osterley Park*, Middx
Isleworth   (020) 8568 7714
This is one of the last great houses with an intact estate in Greater London, set in 140 acres of landscaped park and farmland with ornamental lakes. Originally a c16 mansion (built for Sir Thomas Gresham, founder of the Royal Exchange), it was transformed into neo-classical style by Robert Adam in the c18. Though the house has been a National Trust property for over half a century, the trust only took over the management in 1990. They are currently restoring the gardens, which should be finished sometime in 2001. There is a charge for admission to the house and for car parking.
/ Times: park 9am-7.30pm or sunset if earlier; www.nationaltrust.org.uk; Tube: Osterley; tearoom.

Portobello Road Market W10, W11
1–2B
On Saturday, Portobello market is undoubtedly the place in West London for combining people-watching and browsing. The street market stretches for over a mile, and in fact comprises several different markets. The most famous, the antiques market, is at the south end, but there is also a food market, bric-à-brac stalls and (under the Westway) a good gathering of vendors of trendy clothing and accessories.
/ www.portobelloroad.co.uk; Tube: Notting Hill Gate, Ladbroke Grove.

Ranelagh Gardens SW3
Royal Hospital Rd   3–3D
Apart from when they are cordoned off every year for the famous Chelsea Flower Show (in May), these well-kept gardens lead a rather low-profile life. They are, however, unusually pretty and intimate. A visit here combines well with one to the neighbouring Royal Hospital (see also). / Times: 10am (Sun 2pm)-30 mins before dusk, closed 1pm-2pm; Tube: Sloane Square.

Riverside Walk
See the introduction of the South section for suggestions of interesting walks by the Thames.

Ruislip Woods, Middx
Ruislip   (01895) 250635
There are a number of noteworthy features of these 700 acres of woodland, including the 250-acre Park Wood, the largest unbroken stretch of woodland in London. A particular attraction is the barbecue sites located in the Bayhurst Wood Country Park, another portion of the woods: although there is a charge to book these, you don't have to pay if you are prepared to take pot luck. Ruislip Woodland Centre covers the history of the area, which became a National Nature Reserve in 1997. The centre also gives details of the various species inhabiting the area – there are bats (at dawn and dusk), woodpeckers, warblers and woodcocks to name a few. A short guide to Ruislip Woods is available in local libraries or from the Leisure Service, Education, Youth and Leisure Department, Civic Centre, Uxbridge, Middx UB8 1UW. / Times: woodland centre Sat & Sun 12pm-3.30pm; Tube: Ruislip (then 331 bus); café.

North London

Introduction

North London's unique strength is the way it contains pockets of real nature, which seem to be only a stone's throw from the metropolis itself. The most obvious example is **Hampstead Heath**, but there is also **Highgate Wood** (both accessible by foot from the **Parkland Walk**, see also), and each are within a few tube stops of anywhere in central London.

In addition, there are many fine parks in the area. North London has its own Royal Park, in the form of **Regent's Park**, and its **Primrose Hill** extension which has exceptional views over the city. The northerly **Alexandra Palace Park** gives yet another impressive perspective on the city below. The grounds of **Golders Green Crematorium** are a fine amenity, relatively unknown to those outside the locality.

Few would dispute that Hampstead is by far the finest village in London, and two of its lovely period houses may be visited – **Burgh House** (whose museum gives the history of the area) and Keats House. The village's grandest residence, **Kenwood House**, at the top of the Heath, has an excellent period art collection.

For people who like being among people, the undoubted attraction here is colourful **Camden Market**, which sprawls over the area from the Lock to the tube station every weekend. For children, it's probably the green spaces and the nature which are the main plus point. For the more inquisitive, however, the **Wellcome Trust's** exhibitions (including the **Two10 Gallery**) offer an interesting diversion.

Suggested walk

For a taste of the varied nature of North London, set out for a stroll beginning in Regent's Park at the point where it meets the northern end of Baker Street. Head north – there are maps to guide you – and you will cross the entire width of the park, passing the boating lake to your left, Queen Mary's Gardens and the Zoo. Exiting the main northern entrance of the park, cross Regent's Canal and join Regent's Park Road. This winds along Primrose Hill, offering majestic views of London, as well as of stately houses and tree-lined streets. Continue walking until you reach Chalk Farm Road, with its array of eclectic shops and restaurants. Follow the road south – the activity increases as you reach Camden Lock and, at weekends, the bustling market. If the crowds prove too daunting, sneak down from the bridge at Camden Lock to Regent's Canal and walk east a mile or so to Camley Street Nature Park.

Brent One Stop Shop
Brent Town Hall, Forty Ln   Customer Call Centre
(020) 8937 1200   1–1A
/ Times: Mon-Fri 9am-5pm; www.brent.gov.uk; Tube: Wembley Park.

Camden Direct WC1
Camden Town Hall, Argyle St   (020) 7974 5974
/ Times: Mon-Fri 9am-5pm; www.camden.gov.uk; Tube: Kings Cross.

Harrow Tourist Information Centre, Middx
The Civic Centre, Station Rd, Harrow   (020) 8424 1103
The centre provides detailed information concerning local history, specific places of interest and nature preserves in Harrow. Local maps also are available. / Times: Mon-Fri 9am-5pm; www.harrow.gov.uk; BR: Harrow & Wealdstone.

Indoor attractions

Barnet Museum, Herts
31 Wood St, Barnet   (020) 8440 8066
Wide-ranging local history museum whose three or four annual temporary exhibits include shields from the Battle of Barnet – the penultimate battle in the Wars of the Roses. / Times: Tue-Thu 2.30pm-4.30pm, Sat 10.30am-12.30pm & 2pm-4pm; Tube: High Barnet (then a half mile walk or 184 bus).

Batchworth Lock Centre, Herts
99 Church St, Rickmansworth   (01923) 778382
Batchworth Lock is a historic site on the Grand Union Canal. Located in former stables, the centre provides guides, leaflets and maps showing the network of waterways around Batchworth. One can visit the narrow boats 'Albert' and 'Roger' and even enjoy a 30 minute return trip on the canal to Stockers Lock. Donations are appreciated. / Times: Easter weekend-end Oct Mon, Thu, Fri 10am-3pm, Sat & Sun 11am-5pm; Winter Wed 10am-4pm; www.hertsmuseums.org.uk/info/batchworth.htm; Tube: Rickmansworth.

British Library NW1
96 Euston Rd
(020) 7412 7332, (020) 7387 0626 (recorded info)   4–3C
Does it look like an academy for secret policemen? That was the Prince of Wales's opinion on this striking new building, home to every book published in the UK. You too can form a view of the architecture from the courtyard, but most of the library itself is reserved for those with reader cards. There are, however, two permanent exhibition galleries. The John Ritblat Gallery exhibits over 200 items, including Magna Carta and a Gutenberg Bible. The second is the Workshop of Words, Sound and Images, an interactive gallery that follows book production from the earliest written documents to the digital revolution of our time. On Saturdays, there are free demonstrations of bookbinding, calligraphy and printing.
/ Times: Mon-Sat 9.30am-6pm (Tue 8pm, Sat 5pm) & Sun and bank holidays 11am-5pm; www.bl.uk; Tube: Kings Cross.

Bruce Castle Museum N17

Lordship Ln   (020) 8808 8772

Haringey's museum, with its wide collection of items of local interest, occupies an elegant and striking Grade I listed Tudor manor house. It was also once a school run by a Mr Hill and his sons (one of whom was called Roland), operated on progressive lines (for its day) – for example, there was no corporal punishment and the children were involved in its administration. Roland Hill grew up to be the inventor of the uniformed penny post – a postal history collection reflects his connection with the house. Bruce Castle is located in two acres of parkland, containing a children's playground, bowling green, tennis court and basketball area. An interactive inventor centre has recently been added. Sun 2pm-4pm, there are family activities, and the last Wed evening of each month, there are free talks and events (at 7pm). Past events have included a celebration of Goan culture and a talk about the archaeology of a local farm. Temporary art exhibitions are held from time to time, and during the summer, there are regular arts and crafts activities. / Times: Wed-Fri 1pm-5pm, Sat & Sun 10am-5pm; www.brucecastlemuseum.org.uk; Tube: Wood Green (then 243 bus).

Burgh House NW3

New End Sq   (020) 7431 0144   4–1A

This handsome Queen Anne house (1703) is well worth a visit for its architecture, its pictures and its creaking charm. The ground floor is used as a community centre for the arts and houses temporary art exhibitions. The museum is on the first floor and has displays and objects about the history of Hampstead (long regarded as one of the most desirable places to live in or near the capital) and changing exhibitions on the history of the area. The house makes an ideal stopping-off point between the tube station and the Heath, and in the summer, there is a nice garden to admire. / Times: Wed-Sun (& bank hols) 12pm-5pm; www.heathandhampsteadsociety.org.uk/burghouse.htm; Tube: Hampstead; café.

Camden Arts Centre NW3

Arkwright Rd   (020) 7435 2643   4–2A

The centre's three galleries hold about half a dozen contemporary art exhibitions a year. During shows, there are usually artist-led Sunday talks every two to three weeks. / Times: Tue-Thu 11am-7pm, Fri-Sun 11am-5.30pm; www.camdenartscentre.org; Tube: Finchley Road.

Church Farmhouse Museum NW4

Greyhound Hill   (020) 8203 0130

Built in 1660, this charming building (the oldest hereabouts) combines permanent displays of c19 life – a period dining room (with c17 panelling), scullery (done out as a laundry complete with a display of smoothing irons) and kitchen (with c17 hearth) – with changing exhibitions about local and social history and decorative arts and crafts. / Times: Mon-Thu 10am-12.30pm & 1.30pm-5pm, Sat 10am-1pm & 2pm-5.30pm, Sun 2pm-5.30pm; www.barnet.gov.uk/cultural_services/museums; Tube: Hendon Central.

Crafts Council N1

44a Pentonville Rd   (020) 7278 7700   4–3D

The council is the national body for promoting contemporary crafts, such as pottery, textiles and printing. Its premises include picture and reference libraries as well as a gallery. There are five major exhibitions a year – retrospectives of major artisans or thematic shows of contemporary craft, and there are related events (workshops, lectures, demonstrations) in conjunction with the exhibitions. Recent highlights include exhibitions on weird and wacky spectacles and contemporary jewellery made in Britain. There is also an information service relating to contemporary British crafts. / Times: Tue-Sun 11am (Sun 2pm)-6pm; www.craftscouncil.org.uk; Tube: Angel; café.

Grange Museum of Community History NW10

Neasden Roundabout, Neasden Ln
(020) 8452 8311   1–1A

Brent's community museum, in a converted c18 cottage, includes an Edwardian draper's shop (transplanted from Willesden High Road) and a Victorian Parlour. A permanent exhibition, 'The Brent People', includes a computerised database of local photographs. There is a temporary exhibition space, the Community Gallery, that shows about three or four exhibitions a year. Two computers are set up for free Internet browsing, although it costs money to reply to e-mails or print. This is a child-friendly museum, with 'The Space', which contains a mystery hat and other odd bits for dressing-up, an enclosed garden (with Victorian herb border) open for picnicking, and children's shows, events and activities in the summer. / Times: Mon-Sat 11am (Sat 10am)-5pm (also Sun 11am-2pm in August) ; www.brent.gov.uk; Tube: Neasden.

Harrow Museum & Heritage Centre, Middx

Headstone Manor, Pinner View, Harrow   (020) 8861 2626

Originally built for the c14 Archbishops of Canterbury , this moated manor house has '30s interiors which are still in the course of renovation. It benefits from a pretty setting in a park, and there is also a c18 granary and a large and interesting c16 tithe barn. Here, a Victorian room setting, changing exhibitions and local history displays are on view. There are currently plans to rebuild the ancient parts of Headstone Manor and extend the tithe barn to allow the public better access to the structure. / Times: Wed-Fri 12.30pm (Sat, Sun & bank hols 10.30am)-5pm, closes at dusk in winter; www.harrowarts.com; Tube: Harrow-on-the-Hill (then H14 or H15 bus); café.

Islington Museum Gallery N1
Foyer Gallery, Town Hall, Upper St
(020) 7354 9442   4–2D
It is surprising that Islington – which has undergone a transformation from notorious slum to 'in' part of the capital (forever associated in the public mind with the rise of New Labour) – lacks a fully-fledged local museum. However, in the interim, this volunteer-run gallery is the setting for about five exhibitions a year, exploring the history, sociology, ethnic culture, artistic heritage and architecture of the area.
/ Times: Wed-Sat 11am-5pm, Sun 2pm-4pm; www.islington.gov.uk/localinfo; Tube: Highbury & Islington.

John Perry Wallpapers N1
Cole and Son Wallpapers, 142-144 Offord Rd
(020) 7607 4288   4–2D
TV companies go to this Islington concern for period wallpaper for historic sets such as Pride and Prejudice. *The wall coverings for the Houses of Parliament and Buckingham Palace also originate here. Established in 1875, the company continues to handprint all of its papers using traditional block methods. It can take weeks to print a single roll – fortunately, groups can see several stages of production in one visit!*
/ Times: by appt; www.cole-and-son.com; Tube: Highbury & Islington.

Kenwood House NW3
Hampstead Ln   (020) 8348 1286   4–1A
Perched like a grand wedding cake above Hampstead Heath, this neo-classical house (with Robert Adam façade, 1760s) provides a great cultural climax to a visit to the heath. The house (which was bequeathed to the nation by the first Earl of Iveagh in 1926) is certainly worth a view (the library is reckoned to be one of Adam's finest rooms), as are the artistic treasures within, which include a Rembrandt self-portrait and Vermeer's Guitar Player, as well as many famous works by Turner, Reynolds, Gainsborough, Van Dyck and Frans Hals. There has been a recent refurbishment to the main rooms of the house, including the music room and dining room. If you wander the paths on the estate, you might chance to see sculptures by Henry Moore and Barbara Hepworth. In the summer, open air concerts are held in the bowl by the lake – you can hear them from outside the easy-to-enter enclosure.
/ Times: Apr-Sep 10am-6pm, Oct-Mar 10am-4pm; www.english-heritage.org.uk; Tube: Archway, Golders Green (then 210 bus); café.

Lauderdale House Community Arts Centre*
N6

Waterlow Park, Highgate Hill   (020) 8348 8716   1–1C

The two galleries of this Elizabethan house in the centre of the attractive Waterlow Park hold frequently changing exhibitions. The centre holds regular poetry readings and dance workshops. Entry to the house and galleries is free except when special exhibitions are held. Most shows and workshops are free, although occasionally a fee is charged, so it's generally best to call before you travel. / Times: Tue-Fri 11am-4pm, Sat 1.30pm-5pm, Sun 12pm-5pm (weekends subject to private booking); www.london-northwest.com/lauderdalearts; Tube: Archway (then 143, 210 or 271 bus); café.

International Gallery of Children's Art NW3

255 Finchley Rd   (020) 7435 0903   1–1B

London's only gallery devoted to children's art from around the world. You can check out the current show on their website. / Times: Tue-Thu 4pm-6pm, Fri-Sun 12pm-6pm; www.ligca.org; Tube: Finchley Road.

Museum of Domestic Architecture
& Design 1850–1950 N11

Cat Hill Campus, Middlesex University   (020) 8362 5244

A brand new building was erected on the Cat Hill Campus to house this museum. The core of the six collections here is the Silver Studio, which was one of the leading independent design studios from the 1880s until the 1950s. This collection includes wallpaper and textile designs. Also of note: the library of Sir J M Richards (one of the most important figures in c20 British architectural history and a leading member of the Modern Movement in Britain); the Peggy Angus Archive; the Sir Charles Hasler Collection; the Crown Wallpaper Archive and the British and Domestic Design Collection 1850-1950. / Times: Tue-Sat 10am (Sun 2pm)-5pm; www.moda.mdx.ac.uk; Tube: Oakwood and then shuttlebus (runs every 20 mins) to museum, Cockfosters; café.

National Sound Archive NW1

British Library, 96 Euston Rd   Library (020) 7412 7430, Sound archive (020) 7412 7441   4–3C

This is one of the largest sound archives in the world. The reception area has a touch-screen introduction to the facilities, and you can listen to examples of the material held. You can also pick up free leaflets and a newsletter. There is a library and information service, which includes catalogues of the holdings (both here and, for example, at the BBC) and historical information on recordings. A listening service is also available, by appointment only. The website now has the catalogue database available for viewing. / Times: library & listening service Mon 10am-6pm, Tue-Sat 9.30am-8pm (Thu 6pm, Fri & Sat 5pm); www.bl.uk/collections/sound-archive; Tube: King's Cross, Euston.

Old Speech Room Gallery
Harrow School, Middx

The Old School Building, Church Hill, Harrow-on-the-Hill
(020) 8872 8205, (020) 8872 8000

The Old Speech Room was built in 1819-21 as a place in which to encourage public speaking. In 1976, it was converted into a gallery to exhibit the treasures this famous school has accumulated over the years. There is a nucleus of antiquities plus a series of temporary themed exhibitions which draw on highlights of the collection, such as c19 English watercolours, Modern British painting and some sculpture. / Times: 2.30pm-5pm (closed Wed); closed school holidays; Tube: Harrow-on-the-Hill (then 258 bus).

Shri Swaminarayan Mandir NW10

105-119 Brentfield Rd   (020) 8965 2651   1–1A

The largest outside India (according to the Guinness Book of World Records), this intriguing Hindu temple is a peculiar addition to the skyline of the north-west London suburbs. It was inspired by the c18 guru, Lord Swaminarayan, who walked the length of India preaching the values of social care. The temple was built with the use of 2000 tons of Italian marble and nearly 3000 tons of Bulgarian limestone, which was all shipped to India to be shaped by more than 1000 skilled craftsmen before being shipped to Neasden for assembly, thus being constructed by traditional means. For a small fee, visitors can see an exhibition about Hinduism and watch a 12-minute video show explaining how and why the Mandir (place of worship) was constructed. / Times: 9am-6pm; www.swaminarayan-baps.org.uk/Mandir; Tube: Neasden.

Stables Art Centre & Gallery NW2

Dollis Hill Ln (Gladstone Park)   (020) 8452 8655   1–1A

A contemporary art gallery, housed in the former stables of Dollis Hill House, exhibiting works by local and national artists. / Times: Thu-Sun 11am-6pm (Sep-March 5pm); Tube: Dollis Hill or Neasden.

Stephens Collection N3

Avenue House, 15-17 East End Rd   (020) 8346 7812

In 1918, Henry Charles 'Inky' Stephens bequeathed Avenue House and its grounds to the public. (Stephens Senior was the inventor of the famous blue-black writing fluid that writes blue and dries black, and which because of its indelible nature is still used for signing marriage registers.) Since 1993, Avenue House has housed a collection of artefacts relating to ink and ink products, including original enamel signs, quill and steel-nibbed pens. / Times: Tue-Thu 2pm-4.30pm & by appt; Tube: Finchley Central.

Two10 Gallery NW1

210 Euston Rd   (020) 7611 8888   4–4C

Part of the Wellcome Trust (see also), this science-based art gallery presents about three temporary exhibitions a year. The media vary but the focus is always on exploring the relationship between medical science and art. A past exhibition, 'Shelf Life' peered into our medicine cabinets in a move to clarify myths about our home healthcare. / Times: Mon-Fri 9am-6pm; www.wellcome.ac.uk; Tube: Euston, Euston Square.

Wellcome Trust NW1
183 Euston Rd   (020) 7611 8888   4–4C
The History of Medicine Gallery closed in 1998, and its replacement is still very much under discussion. Until then, however, two smaller exhibitions can be visited within this complex: the Library Reading Room has a small, but regularly changing, exhibition on the history of medicine; and the Modern Medicine Reading Room exhibits pre-1850 objects and printed ephemera from the archives, with themes such as temperance and veterinary medicines. Those interested in the medical theme should combine this visit with a trip to the Two10 Gallery (see also) just across the road. / Times: Mon-Fri 9am-5pm, Sat 9am-1pm; www.wellcome.ac.uk; Tube: Euston, Euston Square.

Outdoor attractions

Abney Park Cemetery N16
Stoke Newington High St   Visitor centre
(020) 7275 7557   1–1C
A surprisingly country-like place (originally laid out as an arboretum), this cemetery that doubles as a nature reserve took over (around 1840) from Bunhill Fields as the final resting place of London's dissenters and non-conformists. General Booth, founder of the Salvation Army, is among those interred here, along with James Braidwood, first Superintendent of the London Fire Engine Establishment. The main entrance has been restored and there is a visitor centre which has information boards covering the geology of the stones of the site, the history and the (mainly local) characters buried here. Throughout the year there are various nature-related events, for which pamphlets can be obtained at the visitor centre or by phone. / Times: summer 9am-7pm, winter 9am-3pm; visitor centre, generally 10am-7pm; www.abney-park.org.uk; BR: Stoke Newington.

Alexandra Palace N22
Alexandra Palace Way   (020) 8365 2121
This 200-acre north London park is made rather special by its panoramic views over the metropolis as well as its historical associations, as the site of the world's first television broadcast in 1936. The popular Grove Shows have been running for a decade – live music every Sunday afternoon between June and August and, during school holidays, high quality performances for kids. Permanent attractions include a children's playground, an animal enclosure (with donkeys and deer) and a conservation area (near the Wood Green entrance). / Times: 24 hours; www.alexandrapalace.com; Tube: Wood Green (then W3 bus or free shuttle service that is available most days).

North London

Camden Lock NW1

Camden High St   (020) 7284 2084   4–2B

*The slightly more upmarket side of Camden Market, with
fashions, jewellery, books and antiques among the enormous
variety of items on display. The lock is open all week, but, as
with the rest of the market, Sat and Sun are the peak times
for a visit. There are frequent summer attractions (generally
during the week), such as street theatre, music and art shows.*
/ Times: 10am-6pm; www.camdenlockmarket.com; Tube: Camden Town,
Chalk Farm; café.

Camden Market NW1

Camden High St (and surrounding area)   4–2B

*At the weekend, the whole of hip young London seems to
descend on Camden for its vibrant markets – together with
the tourists, they make it one of the most visited attractions
in town. (In fact, the Underground stations are closed for much
of the day due to overcrowding, so be prepared to walk, or
know the bus routes!) By no means are prices particularly
bargain basement though, and unless you are shopping for
the latest style, the real point of the trip is to stroll around
window-shopping, people-watching and listening to the
omnipresent musical beats. As with all crowded markets,
keep a close eye on your belongings.* / Times: Thu-Sun 9am-5pm;
www.camdenlock.net/cammarket; Tube: Camden Town, Chalk Farm.

Camley Street Natural Park NW1

12 Camley St   (020) 7833 2311   4–3C

*In the heart of King's Cross – on Regent's Canal (though not
accessible from it) – this community nature reserve is also
a designated Local Nature Reserve. The variety of wildlife
habitats include a marsh, a pond and a wood. Run by the
London Wildlife Trust, it is one of the more than 50 nature
reserves, of varying sizes, within the London area. There are
a few free events here during the year, for example the Spring
Fun Days and the Camley Street Apple Day in October. There
is an ongoing educational programme and a variety of
children's events take place year-round – call for details.
Donations are appreciated.* / Times: Mon-Thu 9am-5pm (or dusk,
if first), Sat & Sun in summer 11am-5pm, in winter 10am-4pm;
www.wildlifetrust.org.uk/london/reserves; Tube: King's Cross.

Coldfall Wood N10

Creighton Ave   (020) 8348 6005

*These 35 acres of ancient woodland to the north of Muswell
Hill are of great ecological interest, and demonstrate examples
of the returning fashion for traditional coppice management.
If you intend to explore, call the Conservation Office who can
provide you with further information, and the leaflet,* Historic
Woodlands in Haringey. / Tube: East Finchley.

Finsbury Park N4
(020) 8802 2612   4–1D
*A large part of the 115 acres of this Victorian park is taken up
with various sports facilities and a boating lake, so there's often
a lot of activity. (You can even go fishing – but there's a charge
for a licence.) There are several playgrounds, and a variety of
small-scale childrens events throughout the year, such as Easter
egg hunts and fireworks night. (For more information about
these, ring the Finsbury Park Action Group on the number
given.)* / Times: dawn-dusk; Tube: Finsbury Park; café.

Freightliners Farm N7
Sheringham Rd   (020) 7609 0467   4–2D
*This three-and-a-half acre city farm in Islington is among the
oldest in London. It has all the usual farm animals, but a less
common attraction is an ornamental garden. The farm hosts
an 'Open Day' on the second bank holiday in May, where the
attractions include sheepdog trials, sheep shearing
demonstrations, country crafts and children's activities.*
/ Times: Tue-Sun 9am-1pm & 2pm-5pm; www.freightlinersfarm.org.uk;
Tube: Highbury & Islington, Holloway Road.

Fryent Country Park NW9
Fryent Way, Kingsbury   1–1A
*For those in search of real country in town, these 260 acres
of unspoilt rural farmland, sandwiched between Wembley and
Kingsbury, are pretty much the perfect answer. Nature walks,
ponds and a wildlife area are among the attractions.* / Times: 24
hours; Tube: Kingsbury, Wembley Park.

Gladstone Park NW10
Dollis Hill Ln   1–1A
*William Gladstone was a frequent visitor to the fine Dollis Hill
House (1824) which forms the centrepiece of this very varied
100-acre park between Neasden and Willesden. Other
attractions include an arboretum filled with hundreds of exotic
trees from all over the world, a pond with ducks and geese,
and an old walled garden.* / Times: 8am-dusk; Tube: Neasden, Dollis Hill.

Golders Green Crematorium NW11
Hoop Ln   (020) 8455 2374   1–1B
*For the casual observer, spring is the time to visit this fine
crematorium, set in 13-and-a-half acres of landscaped grounds.
At that time of the year, the front lawns are covered with
upwards of 100,000 crocuses. Founded in 1902, the building
features unusual northern Italianate architecture (by Sir Ernest
George, RA, who also designed Claridges Hotel). Those who
have been cremated here include Marc Bolan, Gustave Holst,
Charles Rennie Mackintosh, Sigmund Freud, Ronnie Scott, Peter
Cook and Anna Pavlova.* / Times: 9am-6pm (winter 5pm);
Tube: Golders Green; café.

Hampstead & Highgate Ponds NW3
Hampstead Heath
(020) 8348 9945, (020) 7485 4491   4–1A
*Hampstead Heath boasts over 20 ponds – and you can swim
in three of them. During the season (from the first Saturday
before the May bank holiday to the third Sunday in September)
you can choose between the Hampstead Pond (mixed), the
Highgate Pond (men only) and the Kenwood Pond (women
only). Showers and changing areas are available. All ponds
limit children to those aged eight and over, and to one per
adult. Swimmers who do not appear to be 'competent' may
be asked to leave. See also Parliament Hill Lido.* / Times: summer,
mixed 7am-7pm, single sex 7pm-9pm (or sunset if earlier); winter, call to
check; Tube: Hampstead, Kentish Town (then 214 or C2 bus).

Hampstead Heath NW3
(020) 7485 4491   4–1A
*Hampstead Heath's 791 acres, administered by the
Corporation of London, offer everything from a fine c18 house
and art collection with formal gardens – Kenwood (see also) –
to heathland which is as close as you get to real countryside
near central London. There are also tremendous vistas – the
views of the metropolis from some parts of the heath are so
fine they have special legal protection. Other attractions include
the bathing pools (see Hampstead & Highgate Ponds),
concerts at the bandstand on Golders and Parliament Hills,
free talks and walks. For kids there is a playpark, and a
programme of free entertainment including Punch & Judy,
magicians and clowns. A full diary of events is available with
an A5 SAE every March from The Parliament Hill Staff Yard,
Highgate Road, London NW5 1PL.* / Times: 24 hours;
www.cityoflondon.gov.uk; Tube: Hampstead, Golders Green.

Highgate Wood N6
Muswell Hill Rd   (020) 8444 6129
*The 70 acres of Highgate Wood were taken over by the
Corporation of London as "an open space for ever" in 1886.
There's a small playground and a sports ground, but the
attraction is essentially what the name suggests – an ancient
woodland, with diverse flora and fauna, all just a few yards
from the Archway Road. If you're planning to spend more than
an hour or so in the wood, collect or send for a copy of the
free, attractively illustrated booklet, 'Highgate Wood', which
lists the flora, birds and butterflies which can be spotted there.
This, a newsletter and other leaflets on woodpecker trails, bat
conservation trusts and the local natural history are available
from the information hut or with an A5 SAE from Corporation
of London, Highgate Wood, Muswell Hill Road, London N10
3JN. You might also like to explore the neighbouring 48-acre
Queen's Wood (across the Muswell Hill Road), which is
relatively wild and boasts an equally impressive selection of
wildlife. (Both areas are part of the Parkland Walk, see also.)
The information centre organises free walks and talks on an
occasional basis.* / Times: 7.30am-dusk; www.cityoflondon.gov.uk;
Tube: Highgate.

Kentish Town City Farm NW5

1 Cressfield Close, Grafton Rd   (020) 7916 5421   4–2B

A working farm of some four acres, with many typical farm animals and a wide range of activities for children. Opened in 1972, it was the first of its kind to be established and has played an important role in the development of the City Farm movement. / Times: Tue-Sun 9am-5.30pm; www.aapi.co.uk/cityfarm; Tube: Chalk Farm, Kentish Town.

Parkland Walk

(020) 8348 6005

Walking down a railway track might seem a rather hazardous activity, but the redundant line between Finsbury Park station and Alexandra Palace is actually a Local Nature Reserve and offers an interesting alternative for a country walk in town. The total length of the walk is four and a half miles and takes around two hours. It is worth getting the free leaflet (which includes a map, available from the Haringey Conservation Officer on the number given) to avoid getting lost in Highgate Wood or giving up when confronted with the very unpark-like Archway Road. / Tube: Finsbury Park (south section), Highgate (middle), Alexandra Palace; BR or W3 bus back to Finsbury Park (north).

Parliament Hill Lido* NW3

Gordon House Rd   (020) 7485 3873   4–1B

One of London's three remaining lidos, built in 1936, this unheated, open-air pool is open from the first weekend in May to mid-September but is free only for two hours every morning. / Times: Mon-Sun 7am-9am; BR: Gospel Oak.

Primrose Hill NW3

(020) 7486 7905   4–3B

The hill – the 206-ft high continuation of Regent's Park to the north – is by far the most central natural vantage point over London, and is therefore justly celebrated for its views (and is one of the six legally protected viewpoints in the capital). When there's enough snow, it's an extremely atmospheric place to go tobogganing. There has been an outdoor gymnasium on the site since Victorian times and there are still fifteen types of exercise equipment available for year-round use. To get you in the mood, the walk along the towpath of the Regent's Canal from Camden Lock or Little Venice is a nice way of approaching (or leaving) the hill. / Times: dawn-dusk; Tube: Chalk Farm, Camden Town.

Queen's Park NW6
Kingswood Ave   (020) 8969 5661   1–2B
A 30-acre Kilburn park owned and run by the Corporation of London since 1886. It's not particularly large, but popular in this relatively under-provided part of town and especially good for children, thanks to its large, supervised playground and its paddling pool. There is also an ornamental garden and a fine Victorian bandstand. The second Sunday in September sees the annual Queen's Park Day – involving music, comedy, games and a carnival – which draws big crowds. During school holidays, the park offers childrens shows and storytelling events. / Times: 7am-dusk; www.cityoflondon.gov.uk; Tube: Queen's Park.

Railway Fields Nature Park N4
Opposite Haringey/Green Lanes Station
(020) 8348 6005   1–1C
This conservation park, in a former British Rail goods coal yard, has been developed for teaching primary school children about nature. There is a meadow, a woodland and a pond, and even a unique hybrid plant – the Haringey Knotweed. A visitor centre, with leaflets, provides information about the ecology of the site (as well as other places of environmental interest in the borough). / Times: Mon-Fri 10am-5pm (phone to confirm); Tube: Manor House.

Regent's Canal Towpath
Created as part of Nash's design for Regent's Park, these eight or so miles of the Grand Union Canal run from Paddington, along the north of the Park, through Camden at Camden Lock, and on to the waterway's conclusion in Docklands in the east, where it joins the Thames. There is a towpath along its entire length which passes through tunnels and alongside locks, and past the perimeter of parts of London Zoo. The prettiest part is towards its western conclusion in the stretch through Little Venice W9. For the leaflet Explore London's Canals, *send an SAE to British Waterways (London Canals), Toll House, Delamere Terrace London W2 6ND.* / Tube: Camden Town (eastern end), Paddington (west), Warwick Avenue (Little Venice).

Regent's Park NW1
(020) 7486 7905   4–3B
Regent's Park's 297 acres have an atmosphere all of their own, perhaps because the park was in fact designed as a grand garden suburb. In the end, only eight of the 26 villas which John Nash planned at the beginning of the c19 were built (though a few more have been added). Queen Mary's Gardens have one of the finest selections of blooms in the country, including the Eudia, a very rare tree, and the lake boasts an impressive variety of wildfowl.

The annual Music Village (early July) is Britain's longest-running 'festival of living traditions from around the world' and is a platform for international popular music, dance and crafts. During the summer, music is performed on a regular basis at the bandstand or at various other points around the park at weekends and some evenings during the week. There are also children's workshops during school holidays. / *Times: 5am-30 mins before dusk; www.royalparks.co.uk; Tube: Regent's Park, Baker Street, Camden Town, Great Portland Street.*

Roundwood Park NW10
Robson Ave, Harlesden Rd   1–2A
A fine 60-acre Victorian park in Willesden that has impressive floral displays and an aviary stocked with exotic birds. There is also a children's playground. / *Times: 8am-dusk; www.brent.gov.uk; Tube: Willesden Green.*

Waterlow Park N6
Islington   1–1C
Given to the public by Sir Sydney Waterlow in 1889, this 'garden for the gardenless' is situated on a steep hillside and has an unusual three-level lake, formal gardens and terraces. Lauderdale House (see also) is within the park. Facilities include a children's play area. / *Times: 7.30am-dusk; Tube: Highgate.*

South London

Introduction

South London boasts many of the best free destinations, especially for a family day out. Indeed, in **Tate Modern** the area boasts what is now the capital's second most popular attraction.

Just over Chelsea Bridge, **Battersea Park** is the only one of the central parks to benefit from a river frontage, and offers a wide range of attractions. A little further south, **Dulwich Park** is very fine (and, on Friday, can be combined with a visit to the **Dulwich Picture Gallery**). **Crystal Palace Park** is also an interesting destination (especially on a Sunday or a bank holiday afternoon, when the Museum is open).

To the south east – Greenwich – with **Greenwich Park**, the **Royal Naval College** and the **Old Royal Observatory** – makes an excellent destination for a day out, and the **Thames Barrier** is not far away. To the south west, Richmond, and the great adjoining **Richmond Park** is also a very attractive place for a full day's exploration (especially bearing in mind the attractions around Twickenham, just on the other side of the river – see West).

If you're heading back to central London from some of the more grown-up cultural attractions south of the river, such as the **Imperial War Museum**, it's worth bearing in mind that the early evening sees some of London's best free music at the **National Theatre** and the **Royal Festival Hall** – posters on the South Bank list all the free events for the current month.

Croydon Tourist Information Centre, Surrey
Katharine St   (020) 8253 1009
/ Times: Mon-Sat 9am-6pm (Sat 5pm), Sun 2pm-5pm; www.croydononline.org; Tube: Southwark.

Greenwich Tourist Information Centre SE10
Pepys House, 2 Cutty Sark Gardens   (020) 8858 6376
/ Times: Mon-Sun 10am-5pm (reduced hours in winter); www.greenwich.gov.uk; Tube: Cutty Sark (DLR).

Lewisham Tourist Information Centre SE13
199-201 Lewisham High St   (020) 8297 8317
/ Times: Mon 10am-5pm, Tue-Fri 9am-5pm, Sat 10am-4pm; www.lewisham.gov.uk/; BR: Lewisham, Ladywell.

Richmond Tourist Information Centre, Surrey
The Old Town Hall, Whittaker Ave, Richmond
(020) 8940 9125
/ Times: Mon-Sat 10am-5pm, Sun (Easter-Sep) 10.30am-1.30pm; www.richmond.gov.uk; Tube: Richmond.

Southwark Information Centre SE1

6 Tooley St   (020) 7403 8299   5–4C
*This new information point, boasting multi-lingual staff, offers
free leaflets for all the attractions in Southwark. Touch-screen
kiosks and multimedia displays are planned. / Times: Mon-Fri
10am-6pm; Sat & Sun 10am-5.30pm; www.sic.southwark.org.uk; Tube: London
Bridge.*

Riverside Walks

Arguably the finest walking in London, and certainly some
of its best vistas, can be enjoyed on the mostly continuous
paths which run along the Thames, on both the north and
south banks from Kingston in the west to Docklands in
the east. The south bank is, on balance, the better place
to walk, because it is generally more peaceful and it gives
views of the almost invariably more picturesque north
bank. (If you get bored, the distances between bridges are
quite short so you can always swap sides.)

The most rural-feeling of the more central stretches of
the river is the (often muddy) towpath on the south bank
between Putney Bridge and Barnes Bridge. A good route
to try begins at the half-way point, at Hammersmith
Bridge – walk down to Barnes Bridge and circle back on
the north bank (which is also attractive in this area). There
are many good pubs at Hammersmith, some with a river
view, so you might like to time your return to coincide
with lunch.

If it's a walk in the centre of town you're after, there is a
fine continuous stretch between the Houses of Parliament
and Tower Bridge, along Victoria Embankment (the north
bank of the river). In the City the walk leads you past the
picturesque Tower of London to St Katharine's Dock (see
also).

For another stroll on the same stretch of river, one of the
nicest places, not least because it is away from the traffic,
is along the south bank from Westminster Bridge – there
are magnificent views (especially of the Houses of
Parliament and St Paul's) and it is a particularly nice walk
at sunset. One of the best views in London is from the
footbridge built into Hungerford railway bridge (between
Embankment Tube and the South Bank Centre).
Improvements being made to this bridge as we go to press
will soon afford the pedestrian equally splendid views
upriver, towards Parliament, for the first time

Heading east from County Hall and the impressive
Millennium Wheel, you will pass the South Bank Centre
and National Theatre. The daily second-hand book stall
under Waterloo Bridge is a great place to stop and
browse. Beyond this is Gabriel's Wharf – with attractive
gardens and a shopping area, it is particularly busy on

a sunny day – and the ITV television studios. Continue east, past the Oxo Tower, which brings you to the area now known as 'Bankside' – the Tate Modern and the impressive reconstruction of Shakespeare's Globe Theatre are features, as is the (currently unusable) Millennium footbridge, which will eventually be able to deliver walkers directly at the steps of St Paul's Cathedral.

As you near London Bridge, the river path diverts inland, taking you along the atmospheric Clink Street, towards Southwark Cathedral and Borough Market – this area gets quite crowded at weekends. If you wander even further east, you will be able to see Tower Bridge in the distance, and will pass the building site of the new Greater London Authority building, designed by Norman Foster.

Other Thames-side walks to consider include a stroll along the riverside path in Battersea Park (see also), the north bank to the east of Kew Bridge, and, further out of town, the extremely pretty stretch at Richmond, where there is a number of riverside pubs to distract you.

Indoor attractions

Addington Palace, Surrey
Gravel Hill, Croydon   (020) 8662 5000
The Palace – home in its day to six Archbishops of Canterbury – was built in 1776 for Barlow Tregothick, Lord Mayor of London. It is set in a 'Capability' Brown landscape and is of interest both for its architecture and its history. Parts of the Palace were restored in 1900 by Norman Shaw and the décor of the rooms dates from then. The Great Hall is lined with polished Italian walnut and the impressive fireplace is made from Italian marble. Now a conference and banqueting suite, the palace is open seven days a year for guided tours, and to societies on other days by arrangement. / www.addington-palace.co.uk; BR: East Croydon (then 466 bus or no.3 tram); café.

Age Exchange Reminiscence Centre SE3
11 Blackheath Village   (020) 8318 9105   1–4D
The highlight here is the charming '30s general shop with its genuine fittings and original stock. This "hands-on museum of the 1930s and 1940s" should interest anyone who can remember those days, as well as those who cannot. There is a changing temporary exhibition at the rear. The café serves tea and cakes in period style – in the garden in fine weather. / Times: Mon-Sat 10am-5.30pm; www.age-exchange.org.uk; BR: Blackheath; café.

Battersea Arts Centre* SW11

Lavender Hill   (020) 7223 6557   1–4B

The gallery of this busy arts centre, housed in Battersea's fine former Town Hall, holds regularly changing exhibitions. There is generally a charge for the other attractions, but it's worth picking up one of the monthly calendars to look out for the occasional free event. / Times: Mon-Sat 10am-9pm (Mon 6pm), Sun 4pm-9pm; BR: Clapham Junction; café.

Beaconsfield Contemporary Art SE11

22 Newport St   (020) 7582 6465   1–3C

Most exhibitions are free at this contemporary gallery located in the former Lambeth Ragged School in Vauxhall. The gallery sponsors solo installations by artists as well as group shows, sometimes in collaboration with other galleries. / Times: hours vary by exhibition, call to check; www.beaconsfield.org.uk; Tube: Vauxhall.

Bethlem Royal Hospital Archives & Museum, Kent

Monks Orchard Rd, Beckenham
(020) 8776 4307, 8776 4227

Founded in 1247, the original 'Bedlam', Bethlem Royal Hospital, is home to many paintings and drawings by artists who have suffered mental disorder. Some of them were incarcerated here. These include works by artist Richard Dadd (1817-1886), who spent 42 years in criminal lunatic asylums, the dancer Nijinsky, and one Jonathan Martin whose prophetic dreams led him to set fire to York Minster in 1829. In addition, the museum has some material relating to the history of Bethlem. / Times: museum Mon-Fri 9.30am-5pm, but best to check in advance; archives by appt; BR: Eden Park, or East Croydon (then 119, 194, or 198 bus).

Bexley Museum, Kent

Hall Place, Bourne Rd, Bexley   (01322) 526574

The building is part Tudor and part Jacobean and is set in extensive gardens and nurseries. The museum contains displays of local geology, natural history and archaeology, plus a mock-up of a Victorian bath! There are varied temporary exhibitions, mostly on a local history theme, and modern arts and crafts displays. / Times: Mon-Sat 10am-5pm (winter 4.15pm), Sunday 2pm-6pm (summer); BR: Bexley, Bexley Heath; café.

Black Cultural Museum SW9

378 Coldharbour Ln   (020) 7738 4591   1–4C

Every aspect of the history of black people in Britain is covered by the collections of this Brixton museum (in conjunction with Middlesex University). There are also changing exhibitions and displays of work by black artists. Black people have been a permanent part of the population for over four hundred years, but no comprehensive museum yet exists to chart their history: National Lottery funding has been secured to develop these archives and a new site into a larger national museum of black history and culture. / Times: Mon-Sat 10.30am-6pm; Tube: Brixton.

Blewcoat School SW1
23 Caxton St   (020) 7222 2877   2–4C
In 1709, local brewer William Green paid for the building of
this single room. The aim was to provide an education for poor
children, and it was used as a school until 1926. Bought by the
National Trust in 1954, restored in 1975, it is now the Trust's
London Information Centre. / Times: Mon-Fri 10am-5.30pm;
Tube: St James's Park.

Borough Market Open Day SE1
Borough High St   (020) 7407 1002   5–4C
Only established in recent years, this weekly food market has
become a hugely popular Sat (and Fri afternoon) destination.
Food producers from all over the UK (and Europe) set up stalls,
from which you can 'try and buy' goods from cheese to organic
chocolate. It's set within Borough's Victorian (and still-working)
fruit and vegetable market. The very characterful surrounding
area (especially Park Street) has a number of interesting
gourmet food shops, too. Southwark Festival's annual food
festival is also held here (see also). / Times: Fri 12pm-6pm; Sat
9am-4pm; www.londonslarder.org.uk; Tube: London Bridge, Borough.

Bromley Museum, Kent
The Priory, Church Hill, Orpington   (01689) 873826
This local history museum is housed in a largely medieval
building, set in attractive gardens. Exhibitions, which take place
in the Great Hall, include "archaeology of the borough till
Domesday", a social history gallery, the Archaeology Gallery
and a varied programme of temporary exhibitions, including
paintings and crafts by locals. One highlight is Bromley's first
fire engine which dates from the early c19 and a display
commemorating Sir John Lubbock, the first Lord Avebury
(1834-1913), whom we have to thank for bank holidays.
/ Times: Apr-Oct 1pm (Sat 10am)-5pm; Nov-Mar closed Sun & bank hols;
BR: Orpington; café.

Crystal Palace Museum SE19
Anerley Hill   (020) 8676 0700
The museum tells the story of the Crystal Palace, erected in
Hyde Park as a temporary structure for the Great Exhibition
of 1851. The glass building attracted much interest and was
bought and moved to Upper Norwood where it stood until it
burned down in 1936. The museum is housed in a brick-built
part of the original structure. Exhibits are mainly photographs,
including pictures of the fire, as well as some Victorian
souvenirs. The museum is set in 200 acres of parkland – see
also Crystal Palace Park. / Times: Sun & bank hols 11am-5pm;
BR: Crystal Palace.

Cuming Museum SE17

155-157 Walworth Rd   (020) 7701 1342   1–3C

Southwark is one of the most historically interesting parts of London. Its museum (just south of the Elephant & Castle) has a rather unusual basis, being derived largely from the objects collected by the Cuming family between 1786 and 1902. There are five temporary exhibitions a year. Occasionally, there are early evening talks, which may be on a wide range of topics. Special hands-on activities for children, such as dressing up and handling replicas, are held all year round. / Times: Tue-Sat 10am-5pm; www.london-se1.co.uk/attractions; Tube: Elephant & Castle.

Deen City Farm SW19

39 Windsor Ave, Merton Abbey   (020) 8543 5300

Animals at this five-acre city farm range from the expected to rare breeds, and there is also an expanding pure breed poultry programme. The emphasis is on seeing and touching, and there are also information boards, and on weekends, there are barn owl and reptile demonstrations. An upcoming project is the incorporation of a Sensory Garden, which will provide a number of impacts on visitors' senses through sight, smell, touch and hearing. Donations are appreciated. / Times: Tue-Sun 9am-5.30pm; usually open Mons in school hols; www.deencityfarm.co.uk; BR: Wimbledon (then 200 bus to Fips Bridge), Collingswood, South Wimbledon; Tramlink: Morden Road, Fips Bridge; café.

Delfina E1

51 Southwark St   (020) 7357 6600

There are five or six shows per year by contemporary artists in this light and bright gallery, a converted Victorian warehouse in Bermondsey. Works range from paintings to video and film installations. / Times: Wed-Sun 11am-6pm during shows/exhibitions; www.delfina.org.uk; Tube: London Bridge; café/restaurant.

Dulwich Picture Gallery* SE21

Gallery Rd   (020) 8693 5254   1–4C

This is the oldest public art gallery in the UK (1811) and was designed by Sir John Soane. It is almost as notable for its neo-classical design as for its important collection of old masters, which includes works by Rembrandt, Van Dyck, Claude and Poussin. There is a particularly good selection of c17 Dutch art and also some of the greatest portraits by Gainsborough and Reynolds. Perhaps because its scale is not at all intimidating, this is one of the most enjoyable galleries to visit and the building has great atmosphere – in addition, a recent renovation has provided all sorts of new visitor facilities. A curiosity at the gallery's centre is the mausoleum, which contains sarcophagi of the museum's founders. There are three critically acclaimed international loan exhibitions that take place here each year, in spring, summer and autumn (call for details). Combine a visit here with one to Dulwich Park (see also), opposite. / Times: Fri 10am-5pm; www.dulwichpicturegallery.org.uk; BR: North or West Dulwich; café.

Erith Museum, Kent

Erith Library, Walnut Tree Rd, Erith   (01322) 336582
This small museum, on the first floor of Erith Library, features displays of local history, with an Edwardian kitchen and displays about the River Thames and local industries.
/ Times: Mon, Wed & Sat 2.15pm-5pm (Sat 4.45pm); BR: Erith.

George Inn SE1

77 Borough High St   (020) 7407 2056   5–4C
The only remaining galleried coaching inn in London is c17 in origin and was mentioned by Dickens in Little Dorritt. It is still a public house (leased by the National Trust to Whitbread) so anyone can go and have a look at its interior. Parts are extremely characterful and include the tavern clock which dates back to 1745. There are Morris dancing displays in the courtyard in the summer, and at around 8pm on the first Mon of the month (not bank hols) a group plays traditional English music. / Times: Mon-Sat 11am-11pm, Sun 12pm-10.30pm; Tube: London Bridge.

Greenwich Borough Museum SE18

232 Plumstead High St   (020) 8855 3240
The permanent displays at this local museum (housed on the upper floor of Plumstead Library) concentrate on local geology, archaeology, wildlife and local history – it seems the fox and badger displays are particularly popular with younger visitors. More recent periods are represented by collections of household and personal items, and there is a programme of temporary exhibitions. Children's activities are organised on Saturdays (as well as afternoon talks and lectures for adults), and during school holidays – telephone for further information.
/ Times: Mon 2pm-7pm; Tue & Thu-Sat 10am-1pm & 2pm-5pm; BR: Plumstead.

Hall Place & Hall Place Gardens, Kent

Bourne Road, Bexley   (01322) 526574
Hall Place, a Grade I listed country house, was built in 1540 for Sir John Champneis (a Lord Mayor of London), and extended in the c17. Almost all the rooms are open to the public, including the beautiful Great Hall. The building also houses Bexley Museum (see also) and galleries with changing exhibitions. The award-winning formal gardens are laid out on either side of the River Cray and feature a Tudor-style rose garden, a herb garden and a topiary display depicting chess pieces and twelve heraldic animals known as the 'Queen's Beasts'. / Times: Mon-Sat 10am-5pm (winter 4.30pm), Sun & bank holidays 2pm-6pm (winter-not open on Sun); BR: Bexley Village.

Honeywood Heritage Centre*, Surrey

Honeywood Walk, Carshalton   (020) 8770 4297
Alas this c17 house (with Victorian and Edwardian additions), on the edge of the Carshalton Village ponds, is no longer generally free to enter. However, there are at least three days a year when access won't cost you anything. These include the anniversary of the museum (usually the first Sunday in December) and the Heritage Open Weekend (mid-September,

with free tours of the house and gardens). When you do get in you'll find an exhibition setting out the history of the borough (Sutton), including an audiovisual display. Many of the rooms have been refurbished in period style. If you are interested in the changing temporary exhibitions and events, ring for details. / www.sutton.gov.uk/lfl/heritage/honeywood; BR: Carshalton; café.

Horniman Museum SE23

100 London Rd   (020) 8699 1872   1–4D
'Free Museum' is carved in stone at the entrance of this fascinating Forest Hill museum (adjacent to delightful, very well-maintained gardens which boast a bandstand and lovely views over London). A visit here has something for everyone. The building grew out of the enthusiasms of Victorian tea magnate Frederick Horniman, who in 1897 opened this Art Nouveau gallery to house his collection. It is divided into natural history, musical instruments and ethnography, and contains many fascinating exhibits, with an aquarium planned to open in April 2001. There is a good programme of talks and workshops in the museum, arts and crafts every Saturday for children and music in the bandstand in the summer. Note: the main gallery is closed until mid-2002 while it undergoes an extension. / Times: 10.30am (Sun 2pm)-5.30pm; www.horniman.demon.co.uk; BR: Forest Hill.

Hulton Getty Picture Gallery SW3

3 Jubilee Place   (020) 7376 4525   3–3C
The Chelsea gallery of a major photo-library, exhibiting a changing selection of prints. / Times: Tue-Fri 10am-6pm, Sat 12pm-6pm; www.hultongetty.com; Tube: Sloane Square.

Imperial War Museum* SE1

Lambeth Rd   (020) 7416 5000
recorded information (0891) 600140   2–4D
Despite its macho image – which the guns outside the entrance do nothing to dispel – this venue puts on such a variety of displays that every visitor will find something of interest. The heart of the collection, of course, is the fine collection of planes, tanks and every imaginable weapon of war. Using interactive video technology, however, the museum also stages some spectacular exhibits including reconstructions such as the World War I Trench and WWII Blitz Experiences, complete with sounds and smells. Much of the material goes far beyond the 'hardware' of war, with some exhibits telling the human side of the story. The VCGC (Victoria Cross, George Cross) Gallery, for example, displays an array of medals and relates the stories of the people who won them. Recent highlights have included exhibitions of wartime fashion and the Holocaust. The museum presents a fine array of exhibitions geared towards children, some enlivened by actors portraying soldiers and other historical characters. The grounds in which the museum stands – Geraldine Mary Harmsworth Park – are also home to the Tibetan Peace Garden (see also). / Times: 4.30pm-6pm; www.iwm.org.uk; Tube: Lambeth North, Elephant & Castle; café.

South London

Jerwood Space SE1
171 Union St   (020) 7654 0171   5–4B
This 2,600 sq-ft art gallery hosts a year-round programme of one-person and thematic group exhibitions. The gallery is made up of three interconnected spaces and an adjacent outdoor Sculpture Space, and is home to the esteemed Jerwood Painting Prize. / Times: Mon-Sat 10am-6pm, Sun 12pm-6pm; www.jerwoodspace.co.uk; Tube: London Bridge, Southwark; café.

Kingston Museum, Surrey
Wheatfield Way, Kingston upon Thames
(020) 8546 5386
This purpose-built Edwardian museum (dating from 1902) houses three major exhibitions (as well as an art gallery for temporary shows). 'Ancient Origins' illustrates the borough's past from pre-history to Anglo-Saxon times. The newest permanent exhibition, 'Town of Kings', continues the story of Kingston-upon-Thames from the Saxon period to the present. The Eadweard Muybridge Gallery is named after the local Victorian pioneer of cinematography, who proved that trotting horses do have all four hooves off the ground at one time. Highlights of the displays include the original Zoopraxiscope and a panorama of San Francisco from 1878. / Times: Mon, Tue & Thu-Sat 10am-5pm (closed bank hols); www.kingston.gov.uk/museum; BR: Kingston.

Little Holland House, Surrey
40 Beeches Ave, Carshalton   (020) 8770 4781
The Grade II listed interior is one of the attractions of this former home of artist, designer and craftsman Frank Dickinson (1874-1961). Wanting to create a house that would meet with the approval of his mentors, John Ruskin and William Morris, he designed and built the house (in the Arts and Crafts style) and contents himself. Highlights include the painted frieze in the master bedroom, the carved timbers of the living room and the decorated fireplace surrounds. / Times: 1st Sun of month, bank hol Sun & Mon (except in Jan) 1.30pm-5.30pm; www.sutton.gov.uk; BR: Carshalton Beeches.

Livesey Museum SE15
682 Old Kent Rd   (020) 7639 5604   1–3D
Southwark's museum for children presents a lively and varied programme of 'hands-on' exhibitions – past displays have included working robots and optical illusions and anything to do with change, from fashion to science. Exhibitions are directed at the under-12s, but parents and other minders are free to take part. There is a picnic area. / Times: Tue-Sat 10am-5pm (last entry 4.30pm); Tube: Elephant & Castle (then 53 or 172 bus).

London Glass Blowing Workshop SE1

7 Leathermarket, Weston St   (020) 7403 2800   5–4C
The Glass Art Gallery at this well-established glass-blowing studio has three special glass-blowing exhibitions held each year, as well as two exhibitions in other media. Additionally, you are welcome to watch the hand-blown molten glass being blown and transformed into beautiful objects. If you so wish, you can, of course, purchase an example on the way out. There are three open weekends a year, in spring, summer and at Christmas – call for dates. / Times: Mon-Fri 10am-5pm; Tube: London Bridge, Borough; café.

Merton Heritage Centre, Surrey

The Canons, Madeira Rd, Mitcham   (020) 8640 9387
Located in a c17 mansion house in Mitcham, the centre tells the story of the borough of Merton and its people, past and present. There is a changing programme of exhibitions and special events – a past exhibition was entitled 'The Glories and the Dispossessed'. Displays usually include photographic material, artefacts, videos and a 'hands-on' section. / Times: Tue-Sat 10am-4pm (Fri & Sat 5pm), Sun 2pm-5pm; Tube: Colliers Wood (then 200 or 152 bus), Morden (then 118 bus to Vestry Hall), Wimbledon (then 200 bus); Tramlink: Mitcham, Mitcham Junction; café.

Mounted Police Museum, Surrey

Mounted Training Establishment, Imber Court,
East Molesey   (020) 8247 5480
Horses are trained here for public duty and ceremonies. To get to the museum you pass through the stables themselves – the small collection contains artefacts relating to the mounted branch since 1920, with paintings, documents, flags and regalia. / Times: by written appt (groups & clubs preferred); BR: Thames Ditton.

Museum of ... SE1

The Bargehouse, Oxo Tower Wharf, Bargehouse St
(020) 7928 1255   5–3A
The Museum of Collectors, the Museum of Emotions and the Museum of the Unknown ... the name keeps changing at this museum of themed exhibitions located at the ever-popular revived Oxo Tower Wharf. A wander around the design shops of Oxo Tower combines well with a visit to the Museum of ... (see also the riverside walk). / Times: Wed-Sun 12pm-6.30pm; www.london-se1.co.uk/attractions; Tube: Blackfriars, Southwark, Waterloo.

Museum of the Royal Pharmaceutical Society of Great Britain SE1

1 Lambeth High St   (020) 7735 9141   2–4D

The museum traces five centuries' history of medicinal drugs and their use in Britain. It looks at the scientists and traders who invented, developed and sold the potions and pills, and the patients who swallowed them and whose blood fed the leeches. The collection includes eyebaths, enemas, advertisements and c17 apothecary's jars. Changing displays show the rapid development of our understanding of the human body in the c19 and c20 and the impact of new drug therapy on today's society. Non-members must make a telephone appointment with the Curator for a guided tour. / Times: by appt, Mon-Fri 9am-1pm & 2pm-5pm; not public hols; www.rpsgb.org.uk/museum; Tube: Vauxhall, Lambeth North.

Oxo Tower SE1

Barge House St   (020) 7401 3610   5–3A

The free public viewing platform on the eighth floor of this South Bank art deco tower offers excellent views, especially across the river to the City and St Paul's. The building itself is home to the retail studios of artisans such as jewellers, artists, furniture makers and ceramicists, as well as the gallery@oxo, which often has photographic exhibitions. The nearby park is a good place for children to let off steam – you could picnic here or on the benches on the Thames-side promenade between here and the Royal Festival Hall. / Times: studios Tue-Sun 11am-6pm, the.gallery@oxo Mon-Sun 11am-6pm; www.oxotower.co.uk; Tube: Waterloo, Blackfriars, Southwark; café.

Photofusion SW9

17A Electric Ln   (020) 7738 5774   1–4C

This Brixton gallery has monthly-changing shows by leading photographers. / Times: Tue-Fri 9.30am-5.30pm (Wed 8pm), Sat 11am-5pm; www.photofusion.org; Tube: Brixton.

Poverest Road Roman Bath-House & Anglo-Saxon Cemetery, Kent

Poverest Road, Orpington
(01689) 873826 (Bromley Museum)

If you want to get an idea of what it was like to bathe in the early AD years, visit this ancient bath-house, which probably served a small settlement or farm complex between AD270 and AD400. There is a public viewing building from which the excavations can be seen, including a hypocaust (central heating system).

This region's popularity survived the departure of the Romans – pagan Anglo-Saxons buried their dead to the north and east of the Roman ruins, around AD450-AD550; men, women and children were buried with their weapons, jewellery and pottery, which can also be viewed. / Times: by appt; BR: St Mary Cray, Petts Wood.

Public Record Office TW9

Ruskin Ave, Kew, Surrey   (020) 8392 5200   1–3A

This is the national archive of England and Wales – 96 miles of shelving holds records created or acquired by central government and the central courts of law from the c11 until the present day. All the public records previously held at the original Chancery Lane PRO, are now housed at Kew, and this is where you find, for example, the Domesday Book, Jane Austen's will and Guy Fawkes's confessions. There are also temporary exhibitions. An education and visitor centre was recently added. / Times: Mon-Sat 9am-5pm (Tue & Thu 7pm); closed bank hol weekends, public holidays & much of Dec; www.pro.gov.uk; BR: Kew Bridge; Tube: Kew Gardens.

Pumphouse Educational Museum SE16

Lavender Pond Nature Park, Lavender Rd
(020) 7231 2976   1–3D

This building, formerly housing docks machinery, is now home to the Rotherhithe Heritage Museum and is surrounded by a nature park. The museum traces the story of Rotherhithe and its people, as told by objects found on the foreshore of the Thames during 12 years beachcombing by local man, Ron Goode. Objects include coins, clay pipes and dockers' tools. Donations are encouraged. The Nature Park has trails through an orchard, herb gardens and past the 'minibeast city'. Reed beds fringe a pond which is frequented by herons, swans, tufted ducks and dragonflies. For a small fee (£1) a nice activity for kids is the Eagle Watch Club on Saturdays. / Times: Mon-Fri 9.30am-3.30pm; www.se16.btinternet.co.uk; Tube: Rotherhithe, Surrey Quays, Canada Water (from latter two, take the 381 bus).

Puppet Centre Trust SW11

Battersea Arts Centre (BAC), Lavender Hill
(020) 7228 5335   1–4B

The Trust's fine collection of puppets dates from Victorian times to the present. There are also rare photographs, slides, posters and memorabilia. A Library, containing videos as well as books, is open for research. / Times: Mon, Wed & Sat 2pm-6pm, other times by appt; www.sagecraft.com/puppetry; BR: Clapham Junction; café.

Royal British Legion Poppy Factory, Surrey

20 Petersham Rd, Richmond   (020) 8940 3305   1–4A

Each year around 34 million poppies are made here, as is the wreath the Queen lays at the Cenotaph on Remembrance Sunday. The factory was set up in 1922, originally in south east London, to help ex-members of the armed forces who are disabled but who can work to continue to be gainfully employed. Individuals and groups are welcome to join a tour around this working factory. / Times: by appt, Mon-Thu 10am & 1.30pm; Tube: Richmond.

South London

The Royal Festival Hall* SE1
South Bank   (020) 7960 4242   2–3D
The view across the Thames from the upper terrace of the
RFH is one of the finest in London, especially as the sun goes
down. In addition, the concert hall at the centre of Europe's
largest cultural complex offers an extensive range of free
foyer events (all of which are set out in the centre's monthly
programme). There's live music on Wed-Sun, 12.30pm-2pm,
in addition to the regular Commuter Jazz, Fri 5.15pm-6.45pm.
During the summer, there is the Great Outdoors series of
events on the river terraces (and sometimes even on the roof!)

The annual three-week Ballroom Blitz is an opportunity to have
a go at almost any type of dancing. There are workshops
during the day while the events in the evening range from
ceilidhs to '70s disco dancing.

While you're visiting the centre, you can take in one of the ever-
changing art exhibitions in the Festival Hall Galleries, which are
open all day and evening. The Hayward Gallery sometimes
stages free events. / Times: 10am-10.30pm; www.sbc.org.uk;
Tube: Embankment, Waterloo; café.

The Royal National Theatre* SE1
South Bank   (020) 7452 3400   2–3D
Its uncompromising exterior may have taken a while to win
Londoners' affections, but the interior of Sir Denys Lasdun's
riverside building has always found favour with theatre-goers.
Even if you're not going to a show, you can still explore the
various levels of the intriguing layout and view one or more of
the several art exhibitions, which are open all day Mon-Sat.
Or take in the music – it might be early or contemporary,
classical, folk or jazz – at 6pm nightly and 1pm on Saturdays.
/ Times: Mon-Sat 10am-11pm; www.nt-online.org; Tube: Embankment,
Waterloo; café.

Royal Naval College SE10
King William Walk   (020) 8269 4791   1–3D
Wren's baroque Greenwich Hospital (for retired sailors)
became the Royal Naval College in 1873. The extraordinary
Painted Hall (whose entire interior is decorated with paintings
by Sir James Thornhill) should not be missed – the body of
Admiral Lord Nelson was laid in state there in 1806. The
attractive c18 chapel (decorated by James 'Athenian' Stuart)
is also worth a visit. (Services are held every in the chapel every
Sunday at 11am, to which all are welcome.) The Greenwich
Gateway Visitors Centre, at the entrance to the College,
contains a series of exhibitions related to maritime Greenwich,
Tudor Greenwich and Roman Greenwich. / Times: Painted Hall &
chapel Mon-Sat 3.30pm-5pm, Sun 12.30pm-5pm (last admission at 4.15pm);
visitor centre 10am-5pm; www.greenwichfoundation.org.uk; DLR: Cutty Sark
Gardens.

Shirley Windmill, Surrey
Upper Shirley Rd , Croydon   (020) 8656 6037
This five-storey brick tower mill was built in 1859, and last worked in 1892. It was restored in 1998, and retains skeleton sails, its fantail and a Kentish cap. (Note that due to the number and steepness of the stairs the mill is not suitable for the very young or for those who are less than fit.) / Times: Sun from 1st Sun in month from National Mills Day (early May) until 1st Sun in Oct; www.btinternet.com/~new.addington/windmill.htm; BR: East Croydon (then 130 bus); café.

South London Art Gallery SE5
65 Peckham Rd   (020) 7703 6120   1–3D
This elegant Victorian gallery shares its site with the well-known Camberwell College of Arts. It presents a changing programme of innovative contemporary works by international artists. / Times: Tue, Wed & Fri 11am-6pm, Thu 11am-7pm, Sat & Sun 2pm-6pm; www.southlondongallery.org; BR: Peckham Rye, or 36 bus from Victoria, or 12,171 or P3 bus from Elephant & Castle.

Southwark Cathedral SE1
Montague Close   (020) 7367 6700   5–4C
In origin c13 (but with many later alterations), this fine building, just over London Bridge, is a hidden gem. Being rather overshadowed by the fame of the cathedrals on the other side of the river, it benefits from an absence of crowds. It is, in fact, the oldest Gothic church in London (and was apparently the inspiration for Westminster Abbey). Nor does it want for historical associations – the Bard's brother, Edmund Shakespeare, was buried here in 1607, and that same year saw the baptism of university founder John Harvard. At 1.10pm there is an organ recital on Mon and, on Tue, an instrumental music recital. Renovations completed for the millennium added a visitor centre (for which there is a small charge), a refectory and external illuminations. (For information on the exhibitions and special events, ring (020) 7367 6722.) / Times: Mon-Sun 9am-6pm; www.dswark.org/cathedral; Tube: London Bridge; café.

Tate Modern SE1
Bankside   (020) 7887 8000,
recorded info (020) 7887 8008   5–3B
This new national gallery houses one of the world's largest collections of modern art – over 4,000 paintings and 1,300 sculptures. The Tate collection dates from 1900 onwards and, instead of being presented chronologically, is shown in four themed groups: Nude/Action/Body, History/Memory/Society, Still Life/Object/Real Life and Landscape/Matter/Environment. The collection includes important works by Picasso, Matisse, Dalí, Rothko and Warhol as well as contemporary work by artists such as Susan Hiller, Dorothy Cross and Gilbert & George.

Bankside Power Station was transformed into Tate Modern by the Swiss architects Herzog & de Meuron. The Turbine Hall, running the length of the huge building, marks a dramatic and gaping entrance to the gallery. Sir Giles Gilbert Scott (who also famously designed the red telephone box) designed the original building (completed in 1963 and decommissioned in 1981). The new two-storey glass roof at the top of the building allows stunning views of the city from the viewing gallery and café. The top of the chimney is illuminated by the 'Swiss Light'. / Times: 10am-6pm (Fri & Sat 10pm) ; www.tate.org.uk; Tube: Southwark, Blackfriars; cafe.

Vauxhall St Peter's Heritage Centre SE11
310 Kennington Ln   (020) 7793 0263   1–3C
Charlie Chaplin (who was born in the area) is among the subjects of the various local history exhibitions at St Peter's, a classic Victorian Gothic Church, built on the site of the former Vauxhall Gardens. It also houses Victorian paintings, mosaics and carvings. / Times: Tue-Thu 10.30am-4pm; Tube: Vauxhall, Oval.

Wandsworth Museum SW18
The Courthouse, 11 Garratt Ln
(opposite the Arndale Centre)   (020) 8871 7074   1–4B
This local history museum tells the story of Wandsworth from prehistoric times to the present day. There are year-round temporary exhibitions that change approximately every two months, and also worksheets, competitions and holiday activities for children. Highlights are the fossilised skull of a woolly rhino (found under Battersea Power Station), a reconstruction of a wartime shelter and a re-creation of a Victorian parlour. / Times: Tue-Sun 10am (Sun 2pm)-5pm; www.wandsworth.gov.uk/museum; BR: Wandsworth, East Putney (then 37 or 337 bus).

Wimbledon Society's Museum of Local History SW19
22 Ridgway   (020) 8296 9914   1–4B
This small, voluntarily run museum depicts the history of Wimbledon from prehistory to the present day and includes archive material. Until recently, of course, Wimbledon was at a good remove from the metropolis, and its rural past is well illustrated by the collection of watercolours, photographs and prints. Highlights are scale models of local manor houses which no longer exist. / Times: Sat & Sun 2.30pm-5pm; www.wimbledonmuseum.org.uk; Tube: Wimbledon, Putney Bridge (then 93 bus).

Winchester Palace SE1
corner of Clink St & Storey St   5–4C
The c13 town house of the Bishops of Winchester was damaged by fire in 1814, but the remains of some of the walls of the Great Hall, with its unique rose window, still make an impressive ruin today. / www.compassarchaeology.co.uk/medsou.htm; Tube: London Bridge.

Woodlands Art Gallery SE3
90 Mycenae Rd   (020) 8858 5847,
library (020) 8858 4631
*This Georgian house has a great artistic tradition. It was built
for John Julius Angerstein (the 'father of the Lloyds insurance
market'), whose extraordinary accumulation of paintings was,
after his death, acquired by the government to form the basis
of the National Gallery's collection. Woodlands now presents
exhibitions of contemporary art (often by well-known local
artists) which change every month. The building, situated in
a pretty garden, which visitors are encouraged to enjoy, is
shared with the local history library (closed Wed, Fri and Sun),
through whose exhibits visitors are also welcome to browse.
/ Times: Mon, Tue & Thu-Sat 11am-5pm; Sun 2pm-5pm; www.wag.co.uk;
BR: Westcombe Park.*

Outdoor attractions

Battersea Park SW11
Albert Bridge Rd   (020) 8871 7530   3–4D
*This 200-acre park is one of the most popular and most
central family destinations, and rightly so as it's full of things
to look at and do – events are publicised on noticeboards.
The long river frontage (punctuated by the Peace Pagoda given
to the people of London in 1985 by a Japanese Buddhist order)
has lovely views across the river to Chelsea and the Royal
Hospital. Other attractions include the Pump House art gallery,
a herb garden, a deer enclosure and London's largest
adventure playground for 5 to 16 year olds. Excellent literature
is available from the Park Office (to the left of the Albert Bridge
entrance), including 'Introducing Battersea Park' which has
a map, and well-produced tree and nature trail brochures.
There is also a small children's zoo (for which there is a
charge). / Times: 8am-dusk; www.wandsworth.gov.uk/events/evwobp.htm;
Tube: Sloane Square (then 19 or 137 bus); café.*

Beckenham Place Park SE6
Beckenham Hill Rd
(020) 8297 8317 (Lewisham TIC for number)
*Woodland and meadows with walking paths that form part of
the 'Green Chain' (see also). There's also a kite-flying slope and
sports facilities (golf course, putting green and tennis courts).
/ Times: dawn-dusk; www.beckenham.net/parks/place; BR: Ravensbourne,
Beckenham Hill.*

Bermondsey Antiques Market SE1
Bermondsey Sq   1–3C
*If you arrive at dawn, you'll have missed the best bargains at
London's largest antiques market (so take a torch and dress
warmly). As the sun rises, the professionals depart and the
trippers take over. / Times: Fri 5am (or earlier)-1pm; Tube: Night buses
N53 (from Trafalgar Square), or later Borough or Elephant & Castle; café.*

Blackheath SE3
1–4D

For centuries the heath was wild and a popular haunt for highwaymen. Now, this large, flat expanse of grass which separates the pretty village of Blackheath from Greenwich Park is well-known for its annual Kite Festival (see Events). There are a couple of ponds (one for boating), but generally its attraction is as a big, open space for running about on. A visit here would combine well with one to the Age Exchange Reminiscence Centre (see also). / BR: Blackheath.

Brixton Market SW9
Brixton Station Rd   1–4C

The characterful warren of streets and alleys around Brixton tube houses as exotic a market as you will find in London, with food and fabrics from Africa and the Caribbean, as well as the mundane items you expect to find anywhere. / Times: Mon-Sat 8am-5.30pm (Wed 1pm); Tube: Brixton; café.

Chumleigh Gardens SE5
Chumleigh St, Burgess Park   (020) 7525 1050   1–3C

Tucked away, behind high walls in the bland expanses of Burgess Park is a collection of erstwhile almshouses (from 1821) and a multi-cultural garden. The garden is divided into areas: Afro-Caribbean, English, Islamic, Mediterranean and Oriental, and all flora are labelled. There are also two ponds. Owing to the water, and the poisonous or spiny nature of some of the plants, kids should not be allowed to explore unaccompanied. / Times: Tue, Thu & Sun 2pm-4pm (other times by arrangement); Tube: Elephant & Castle (then P3, 185, 176 or 40 bus); BR:Denmark Hill (then 42 bus); café & picnic area.

Crystal Palace Park SE19
Sydenham   (020) 8778 7148

The Crystal Palace was an enormous glasshouse which served as a hall at the Great Exhibition of 1851 before being dismantled and moved to Norwood, where it was consumed by fire in 1936. There's a small museum about it (see also). However, there is much more to this large and attractive park than just historical associations. The permanent free attractions include a maze, a children's play area and a unique collection of full-scale Victorian models of dinosaurs. Regular events include the annual Victorian Day (usually the last weekend in June). Over the May Day bank holiday there is also an annual vintage car rally. During the Easter and summer school holidays there are special events for kids, some of which are free. Year-round you can follow the Tree Trail – details about this and other events can be obtained from the Information Centre (at the Penge entrance) on the number above. Note: there are renovation works going on until the beginning of 2002, and as a result, various parts of the park may be closed. / Times: 7.30am-dusk, information centre 9am-5pm; BR: Crystal Palace.

Cutty Sark* SE10
Cutty Sark Gardens by Greenwich Pier
(020) 8858 3445   1–3D
*This famous tea clipper, built in 1869 at Dunbarton, is the only
one that remains in existence today. It has been in Greenwich
since 1954 in a special dry dock. If you visit around lunchtime,
you will hear the cannon that is fired on deck every day at
1pm. Unfortunately, there is a charge for visits to the interior.*
/ www.cuttysark.org.uk; DLR: Cutty Sark, Greenwich.

Danson Park, Kent
Danson Rd, Welling   (020) 8304 2631
*The park was landscaped in the style of Capability Brown and
features an ornamental seven hectare lake. The park lends
itself to a wide range of recreational activities, particularly on
the lake. In the summer, boat races are a popular spectacle,
and in July there is a festival and a series of outdoor concerts.
The park surrounds the c18 Danson Mansion, which was
designed by Sir Robert Taylor, architect of the first Bank of
England. The Mansion is being renovated by English Heritage
and will open to the public in 2001. At the time of going to
press, it was not determined if there would be an entrance fee.*
/ BR: Bexley Heath, Welling.

Dulwich Park & Belair Park SE21
College Rd   (020) 7525 1554   1–4C
*A fine collection of trees is the particular attraction of this fine
75-acre Victorian park. The rhododendrons and azaleas are
a beautiful feature and for these May is the time to visit.
The Park Ranger service (tel (020) 8693 5737) organises
walks (such as bat-spotting on summer evenings) and talks
throughout the year, and produces a quarterly events
programme. The neighbouring Belair Park, of 30 acres, is
relatively little known, but worth looking at, having been laid
out in the late c18 in the classic English landscape style. You
can combine a visit to both with a trip to the Dulwich Picture
Gallery (see also) or the Horniman Museum (see also).*
/ Times: 8am-dusk; BR: North or West Dulwich.

Foots Cray Meadows, Kent
Bexley   (020) 8304 2631 (Danson Park)
*This rural area of woodland and open parkland follows the
course of the River Cray, and is home to an abundance of
wildlife – bird-watchers often visit in hopes of seeing
kingfishers. There is a bridal path and the remains of Foots
Cray Place, a Palladian mansion built in 1756, but destroyed
by fire in 1949. (The walled garden and stable block survived.)
Five Archers Bridge, across the Cray, is also worth a look*
/ BR: Bexley Heath, Welling.

Green Chain Walk

The Green Chain Walks are a twisting network of over 15 miles of well-signposted routes. They link many of south east London's finest parks and open spaces into walks which contain as much greenery as possible. Four leaflets detailing the walks – (Thamesmead or Erith to Oxleas Wood; Thames Barrier to Oxleas Wood; Oxleas Wood to Mottingham; and Mottingham to Crystal Palace or Chislehurst Common) – are available from South East London libraries and Tourist Information Centres.
/ www.greenchain.com

Greenwich Markets SE10

(020) 8293 3110   1–3D

If you enjoy nosing around market stalls, it's well worth making a special weekend journey to Greenwich, which has what is possibly the most comprehensive – as well as the most attractively situated – series of marketplaces in London. The individual markets are: Bosun's Yard (crafts), Greenwich Church Street; the Antiques Market, Greenwich High Road; the Central Market (general), Stockwell Street; and the Craft Market – the original market (1837) formerly a collection of fruit and veg stalls but now selling arts and crafts. The Open Air Food Market, located at the side of the National Westminster Bank, sells home-baked breads, organic foods and hot oriental meals.
/ Times: Sat & Sun 10am-5pm, summer sometimes Fri; BR: Greenwich; café.

Greenwich Park SE10

(020) 8858 2608   1–3D

These 183 acres, enclosed in 1433, constitute the oldest of London's Royal Parks. It was popular with Henry VIII, who was born locally and who held jousting tournaments here every year. It is one of the best outdoor venues, still offering something to entertain all the family. There are red and fallow deer in the deer park (established here in the c15), flower gardens and a children's playground. Brass bands play at the bandstand on Sunday afternoons and evenings during the summer – picnicking by the audience is encouraged. In May and July, there are family events. There is also a free summer football school during school holidays (Charlton Football Club tel: 020 8850 2866). The view from the top of the hill by the Old Royal Observatory (see also) is quite something, and don't miss the Information Centre (at the St Mary's Gate entrance) which has rooms explaining the history and wildlife of the park.
/ Times: dawn-dusk; www.royalparks.co.uk; DLR: Cutty Sark, Greenwich; café.

Lesnes Abbey Woods, Kent
Abbey Rd, Belvedere   (020) 8312 9717
Taking its name from the c12 abbey whose remains still stand, this 200-acre wood, together with the adjoining Bostall Heath and woods (160 acres), makes up one of the largest areas of trees in south London. The spring sees a tremendous show of wild daffodils, and then wood anemones and bluebells. A rather unusual attraction is the natural fossil bed, in which the public can search for shark and ray teeth, and shells. The woods are quite hilly and it's a good idea to take stout footwear. An information centre has been added adjacent to the ruins, and from here, you can pick up literature on self-guided trails. / BR: Abbey Wood.

London Wildlife Garden Centre SE15
28 Marsden Rd   (020) 7252 9186   1–4D
For those looking for special gardening secrets – making an area attractive to butterflies or how to cover a wall in ivy – this is the place to go. The centre offers assistance with all matters of natural, wildlife gardening. For extensive help, workshops take place regularly. / Times: Tue-Thu & Sun 10.30am-4.30pm; BR: East Dulwich, Peckham Rye.

Morden Hall Park, Surrey
Morden Hall Rd   (020) 8648 1845
This informal 125-acre park, owned by the National Trust, was laid out around 1860 as a deer park. It is given additional interest by a complex network of waterways coming off the River Wandle (which were designed to be partly ornamental and partly to power the snuff mills which still stand), as well as the two acre rose garden which boasts 2,000 rose bushes when in full bloom. You can also visit the three craft workshops and watch local artists and artisans at work. / Times: dawn-6pm; craft workshops 10am-5pm, daily except Tue (& Wed sometime); www.nationaltrust.org.uk/regions/southern/Morden.htm; Tube: Morden; café.

Old Royal Observatory* SE10
Greenwich Park   (020) 8858 4422   1–3D
You can bestride two hemispheres at the top of the hill in Greenwich Park. There's a charge to go inside the charming c17 Observatory (which has one of London's few surviving Wren interiors), but the 0 degrees longitude line is marked outside as well. Many people consider that being photographed with one foot in the western hemisphere, and the other in the eastern, is an obligatory souvenir.

The Observatory is the spiritual home of the Greenwich Time Signal. A longer-established visual sign of time passing is the red ball on top of the Observatory, which descends its pole at 1pm every day – its original purpose was to enable seafarers to set their chronometers correctly, which was essential if they were to be able to locate themselves on long sea journeys.

The view from outside the Observatory is possibly the best in London and also summarises the history of London. Immediately ahead, you see the city's imperial past (the Royal Naval College), to the west sprawls the City and central London, and across the river looms the future, in the form of the burgeoning towers of Canary Wharf. / Times: dawn to dusk; www.rog.nmm.ac.uk; DLR: Greenwich.

Oxleas Woods SE18

Shooters Hill, Eltham   (020) 8319 4253

One of the capital's last remaining ancient woodlands (some 8,000 years old) was saved from the road-builder's bulldozer in the late 1980s. The wood supports over 33 different species of tree and shrub, including the rare wild service tree, the hornbeam and guelder rose. Fungi proliferate, with more than 200 species, including the 'storybook' toadstool, the poisonous fly agaric (red with white spots). Worth a glance is Sevendroog Castle, a folly that was built as a memorial to Sir William James Bart in the 1780s. The wood forms part of the Green Chain Walk (see also). There is parking within the woods, accessible from Shooters Hill (A207) and some of the other surrounding roads. / BR: Falconwood; cafe.

Richmond Park, Surrey

Holly Lodge, Richmond (office address)
(020) 8948 3209   1–4A

This enormous park (2,500 acres) was created by Charles I by enclosing farmlands, and was used as his hunting park. Some remains of Richmond Palace – the gateway on the Green and the restored Wardrobe buildings – can still be seen. The park has changed little in the last 300 years, and still contains some 700 red and fallow deer. Because it has been disturbed very little, the park offers some rare natural habitats and has been declared a Site of Special Scientific Interest and, in 2000, a National Nature Reserve. The Isabella Plantation (towards the Kingston Gate) is noted for its fabulous collection of azaleas, and views from King Henry's Mound (which may have been a Bronze Age burial 'barrow') stretch as far as the City.
/ Times: pedestrians 24 hours; vehicles dawn-30 mins before dusk; www.royalparks.co.uk; Tube: Richmond.

Surrey Docks Farm* SE16

Rotherhithe St   (020) 7231 1010   1–3D

This well-equipped city farm is in a slightly away-from-it-all and picturesque location, on the banks of the Thames opposite Canary Wharf. In addition to all the usual animals, attractions include an orchard, a blacksmith's forge, a nomadic Mongolian felt tent, a herb garden, beehives and a bee room – it is possible in the autumn for kids to help collect the honey. Family visits are free but there is a charge for groups. / Times: Tue-Sun 10am-5pm (Sat & Sun closed 1pm-2pm); school hols closed Mon-Fri 1pm-2pm; Tube: Rotherhithe; café.

Sydenham Hill Wood Local Nature Preserve SE26
Crescent Wood Rd   (020) 8699 5698   1–4D

This preserve of rare and ancient woodlands, some more than 400 years old, faced imminent destruction before the London Wildlife Trust took control in 1982. The area covers over 50 acres and is home to some 200 species of wildflowers and trees, as well as over 50 species of birds and mammals. The preserve also includes relics of an impressive Victorian garden, a remnant of a c19 estate. / www.wildlifetrust.org.uk/london; BR: Sydenham Hill.

Thames Barrier Park E16
North Woolwich Rd

London's first new urban park for 70 years, designed by a French landscape designer Alain Provost. Features include a 3km trench, 5m deep, to provide a microclimate for plants, and a riverside promenade.
/ Times: dawn to dusk; Tube: Silver Town (DLR).

Thames Barrier* SE18
1 Unity Way   (020) 8854 1373

The Thames Barrier is the largest movable anti-flooding protection device in the world – it was built in response to the ever-greater threat posed to low-lying central London by high tides (which have been rising at the rate of about 75cm a century). The barrier spans the 520m Woolwich Reach and consists of 10 separate, massive, movable steel gates.

The most spectacular time to visit is during the annual all-day test (in September or October), when the entire barrier blocks the high tide, but it's an impressive sight at any time. (There are also monthly closures, but these happen as early in the morning as possible to minimise closure of the river.) There is a charge for the visitors centre, but not for access to the riverside walk or the children's play area.
/ www.greenwichinfo.com/tourism/barrier.htm; BR: Charlton.

Tibetan Peace Garden SE1
St George's Rd
(020) 7930 6001 (Tibet Foundation)   2–4D

This charming garden, situated in a park shared by the Imperial War Museum (see also), was dedicated in May 1999 by His Holiness the Dalai Lama. The centrepiece is the language pillar, containing a message of peace in four languages – Tibetan, English, Hindi and Chinese. The garden's design incorporates the fundamental Buddhist image, the Wheel of Dharma, and contains sculptures, a bronze cast and native Himalayan and Tibetan plants.
/ www.tibetanpeacegarden.com; Tube: Lambeth North, Elephant & Castle.

South London

Vauxhall City Farm SE11
24 St Oswald's Place   (020) 7582 4204   1–3C
It may be less than an acre in size, but this tiny farm, run on a voluntary basis, boasts a full range of farm animals. Look out for rabbits, geese, ponies, donkeys and sheep. / Times: Tue, Thu, Sat & Sun 10.30am-1pm & 2pm-4.30pm; Tube: Vauxhall; café sometimes, Sun 2pm-4pm.

Well Hall Pleasaunce SE9
Well Hall Road, Eltham
A rose garden, a stream and a waterfall, as well as a moat and colourful flowerbeds are among the features of this unusual park, surrounding a c15 Tudor barn (now a restaurant).
/ www.greenwich.gov.uk.

Wimbledon Common SW19
(020) 8788 7655   1–4B
The common – as everybody knows, home to the Wombles, who keep it clear of rubbish – extends to nearly two square miles, some of which is quite rough countryside, and there are several ponds with much birdlife. It is the setting for one of London's few remaining windmills, which now houses a museum (Apr-Oct) about the history of this type of machinery, complete with working models, for which there is a charge, albeit a small one. A new addition is a wheelchair track that allows those on wheels to cover part of the common.
/ Times: pedestrians 24 hours; vehicles sunrise-sunset; www.wpcc.org.uk; Tube: Southfields, Wimbledon; café.

Woolwich Foot Tunnel
North Woolwich Pier, New Ferry Approach   (020) 8854 8888 ext 5493 (to confirm lift times)
Another chance to walk under the Thames (see also Greenwich Foot Tunnel) which combines nicely with a trip over the river, on the Woolwich Free Ferry (see also). / Times: lift service, Mon-Sat 7am-6pm, Sun 9am-4.30pm; tunnel 24 hours unless there is major maintenance work; BR: north of the Thames, North Woolwich; south of the Thames, Woolwich Arsenal, Woolwich Dockyard, or 180 bus to Greenwich.

The City

The City

Introduction

The tiny, but very wealthy Square Mile is often likened to a city-state. It has its own ways of doing things which have been arrived at over practically a millennium of running its own affairs, and its long history has left it rich in historic buildings and institutions. Its wealth and importance are symbolised by its medieval **Guildhall**, where great banquets for foreign heads of state are often held, and by the great cathedral of St Paul's – other great sights include the **Tower of London**, **Tower Bridge** and the **Monument**.

Trading and, later, banking were the foundations of the City's wealth. Today more international banks gather together in the City than anywhere else. Sadly, most trading and banking business nowadays happens over the telephone, and sometimes without any obvious human intervention at all. For the casual visitor, the **Bank of England Museum** provides the only insight into these sadly now rather closed worlds. If you want to see institutions at work, the barristers' **Inns of Court** are some of the most interesting, picturesque and immutable of all – and most are open to the public to a greater or lesser extent.

The City also has indoor attractions on its fringes, such as the **Mount Pleasant Sorting Office** and the **London Silver Vaults** – both of which should be of interest to older children and adults.

If planning a visit, it's a good idea to arrive in the late morning and begin by visiting the City Tourist Information Office – there is usually at least one free lunchtime concert in one of the City's fine churches (many designed by Wren).

Suggested walk

An afternoon walk through the City, leads one through 1,000 years of London history. Begin at Tower Bridge and the Tower of London. Move west along Tower Street, which becomes Eastcheap, until reaching Monument, to learn about the Great Fire of 1666. Next, an interesting stop would be the Bank of England Museum. Follow King William Street north and west until it meets Threadneedle Street. The Bank is ahead of you, and the entrance to the museum is on Bartholomew Lane, to your right. From the museum you have two options. One is to head south along Queen Victoria Street until reaching St. Peter's Hill.

Descending the steps to the Thames brings you to the foot of the new Millennium footbridge, which – once re-designed to stop it wobbling – will connect the City with the new Tate Modern gallery at Southwark (see also). Alternatively, you can head west from the Bank of England along Cheapside to St Paul's Cathedral. From here, it's not far to the Barbican. If you time your walk correctly – concluding around 5.30pm – you'll be able to take in an early evening performance in the foyer of the concert halls.

City of London Information Centre EC4

St Paul's Churchyard   (020) 7332 1456   5–2B
The City has a conveniently positioned general tourist information centre right by St Paul's. It has copies of City Events, *an excellent guide to the musical and other events happening in the City during that month.* / Times: 9.30am-5pm (Sat 9.30am-12.30pm, closed Sun); www.cityoflondon.gov.uk; Tube: St Paul's.

Liverpool Street Station Tourist Information Centre EC2

5–2D
The office is in the approach to the Underground station.
/ Times: Mon-Sat 9am-6pm, Sun 9.30am-5pm; Tube: Liverpool Street.

Indoor attractions

Bank of England Museum EC2

Bartholomew Ln   (020) 7601 5545   5–2C
Housed within the forbidding building of the Bank itself, the museum is at the very centre of the City of London and traces the history of the Bank from its royal foundation in 1694 right up to the present. There are four DVD interactive videos which help bring the institution's activities to life by telling the role of the bank today as well as the history of bank note design and production. The museum has gold bars and a copy of every bank note the Bank has ever issued. Curiosities include documents relating to George Washington (a former customer), Kenneth Grahame (a former Secretary of the Bank, as well as being the author of The Wind in the Willows*) and the original cartoon by James Gillray which famously satirised the Bank as the 'Old Lady of Threadneedle Street'. The neo-classical Bank Stock Office by Sir John Soane, recreated for the museum, makes a graceful centrepiece and is used for temporary exhibitions.* / Times: Mon-Fri 10am-5pm; also day of the Lord Mayor's Show (2nd Sat in Nov, see also); www.bankofengland.co.uk; Tube: Bank.

Barbican* EC2
Silk St   (020) 7638 4141   5–1B

Love it or hate it, the City's sprawling, concrete arts and residential complex is undoubtedly impressive, with its vast concert hall, theatre, cinema and sweeping internal spaces – the biggest arts centre under a single roof anywhere in the world. There are FreeStage events in the foyer (anything from jazz to Irish folk music) most days between 5.30pm and 7.15pm (and also most Suns 12.30pm-2.30pm) – see the centre's programme for details – and there are often special themed events on bank holiday weekends. Free displays of local interest take place in the library foyer where local artists let the space for six weeks at a time, arts exhibitions in the Concourse Gallery and other works in the Foyer Gallery, in addition to the work shown in the Craftspace and Jewellery Case.
/ Times: 8.30am (Sun 12pm)-11pm; library Mon-Sat 9.30am-5.30pm (Tue 7pm, Sat 12pm); Concourse Gallery Mon-Sun 10.30am (Sun 12pm)-7.30pm; bank hols 12pm-6pm; www.barbican.org.uk; Tube: Barbican, Moorgate; café.

Chartered Insurance Institute EC2
20 Aldermanbury   (020) 7417 4425   5–2C

The Institute's very characterful building (near the Guildhall) houses displays illustrating the history of insurance through the ages. The main hallway (not generally accessible to the public) houses the world's largest collection of firemarks – the metal plaques which, in earlier times, indicated that a building was insured, and by whom. However, there is also a small museum that tells the history of insurance and houses an old fire engine. The building dates from the 1930s and, ironically, it was the only building in the area that wasn't bombed in the Blitz. It's a good idea to phone before you set out. / Times: Mon-Fri 9am-5pm, but phone first to check the areas are not under private hire; www.cii.co.uk; Tube: St Paul's, Moorgate.

The Clerks' Well EC1
14-16 Farringdon Ln   (020) 7527 7960   5–1A

The source that gave the surrounding area of Clerkenwell its name was subsequently filled in and built over. However, the well chamber can still be visited – you can see an iron pump and plaque from 1800, some c16 refacing work and a later wall probably from the c17. Access is by key from the local library, see details below. Groups – 4 to 15 people – preferred.
/ Times: Mon, Tue & Thu, by appt with the attendant from Finsbury Public Library, 245 St John Street, EC1, tel: (020) 7527 7960; Mon & Thu 9.30am-8pm, Tue & Sat 9.30am-5pm, Fri 9.30am-1pm; Tube: Farringdon, Angel, Barbican.

Clockmakers' Company Collection EC2

Guildhall Library, Aldermanbury   (020) 7332 1868   5–2C
*The Clockmakers' Company may go back only to 1631, but
its collection of clocks dates from the c14. This single room
museum contains a glittering and fascinating selection of
timepieces including curiosities, such as the first electric clock
and a timepiece powered by gas. There is also a large silver
watch reputed to have belonged to Mary Queen of Scots, and
the one worn by Edmund Hillary during his ascent of Everest
in 1953. To hear the collection at its best, make sure you are
there at noon. Note: the collection is closed until August or
September 2001 for refurbishment.* / Times: Mon-Fri
9.30am-4.45pm; Tube: St Paul's.

College of Arms EC4

Queen Victoria St   (020) 7248 2762   5–3B
*The College, which traces its origins to the c13, is the body
empowered by the sovereign to determine everything relating
to the granting of new coats of arms and the right to bear
arms which have been granted in the past. The main part of
its building is c17, while the impressive wrought iron gates
came from a country house and were given by an American
benefactor. The Earl Marshal's Court Room is one of the finest,
secular, period rooms in the City to which the public has
access.* / Times: Mon-Fri 10am-4pm; www.college-of-arms.gov.uk;
Tube: Blackfriars, St Pauls.

Family Record Centre EC1

1 Myddelton St   (020) 8392 5300   5–1A
*If you want to trace your family history, you can now find
microfilms of census, probate wills and non-conformist registers
(formerly at Chancery Lane) and Birth, Marriage and Death
Registers (previously at St Catherine's House) on one site in
Islington. Benefits of the move include larger-capacity reading
rooms and bigger refreshment areas. To apply for certificates,
you need a document such as a driving licence or cheque card
with your signature on it, or if you are not British, your passport
or national identity card.* / Times: Mon & Wed-Fri 9am-5pm (Thu 7pm),
Tue 10am-7pm, Sat 9.30am-5pm; closed bank hol weekends & public holidays;
www.pro.gov.uk/about/frc; Tube: Angel, Farringdon.

Guildhall EC1

Gresham St   (020) 7606 3030   5–2C
*The hall on this site has been the most important secular
building in the City since the c11 – many important events and
glittering state banquets take place here. Much of the present
building (which is on a spectacular scale) dates from 1440,
and, although fire and bomb damage have taken their toll,
a fair amount of the original remains. The magnificent hall is
usually open to casual visitors (ring to check), and pre-booked
parties (10-50 people) may also visit the Old Library and the
medieval crypt.* / Times: May-Sep, Mon-Sun 10am-5pm; Oct-Apr, closed
Sun; www.cityoflondon.gov.uk/history; Tube: St Paul's, Bank.

The City

Guildhall Library EC2
Aldermanbury   (020) 7332 1868   5–2C
*This elegant library specialises in the history of London. If this
is an area which interests you, this is a delightful place to
while away a couple of hours. Information not available on
the shelves can normally be retrieved from the stores within
10 minutes. There is an area where visitors can consume
packed lunches.* / Times: Mon-Sat 9.30am-5pm (restricted service Sat);
Tube: Moorgate, Bank, St Paul's.

Livery Halls EC1
*The proud and ancient livery companies of the City boast
a large number of halls some of which are extremely grand
and historic. Gaining access to most of them is difficult, but
it is worth applying to the City Information Office early in each
year for part of the small allocation of tickets which they
receive every February. The companies participating in the
scheme vary, but have recently included the Goldsmiths, the
Tallow Chandlers, the Skinners, the Fishmongers, the
Ironmongers and the Haberdashers. Groups of up to 30 can
arrange an appointment to be shown around the magnificent
Fishmongers' Hall at other times by contacting the archivist on
(020) 7626 3531, ext 257. (Note that the hall is closed from
the end of July to the end of September.) The Corporation of
London website (www.cityoflondon.gov.uk) has links to all the
major livery company websites.*

London Metropolitan Archives EC1
40 Northampton Rd   (020) 7332 3820   4–4D
*The name says it all. For anyone interested in the history
of London (and Middlesex) – or wanting to research their
Londoner forebears – this City-fringe establishment offers
a fascinating glimpse at city life in past centuries. There are
documents, books, maps and photographs – many on open
access, but some available only upon request, the earliest
documents dating from c15.* / Times: Mon-Fri 9.30am-4.45pm (Tue &
Thu 7.30pm); www.cityoflondon.gov.uk/archives/lma; Tube: King's Cross,
Farringdon, Angel.

London Silver Vaults WC2
Chancery House, Chancery Ln   (020) 7242 3844   2–2D
*This intriguing, subterranean shopping mall, with its 38-40
silver dealers, claims to offer the largest collection of silverware
under one roof in the world. All the items are for sale, with
prices ranging from £5 to £500,000, but you're quite welcome
just to go and browse.* / Times: Mon-Fri 9am-5.30pm, Sat 9am-1pm;
Tube: Chancery Lane.

Museum & Library of the Order of St John EC1

St John's Gate, St John's Ln   (020) 7253 6644   5–1A

The ground floor of St John's Gate houses the historic collections of the Order which include Maltese silver and furniture, pharmacy jars, paintings, prints, drawings and arms and armour. All items reflect the history and work of the Knights Hospitaller from the time of the Crusades to the present day. Tours can be arranged which take in the Museum but also the rest of St John's Gate (see also). The reference library is open by appointment on Saturday. / Times: Mon-Fri 10am-5pm, Sat (library by appt, exhibition rms 10am-4pm); www.sja.org.uk/history; Tube: Farringdon.

Museum of London* EC2

London Wall   (020) 7600 1058   5–2B

One of London's most interesting and best presented museums offers 14 galleries of permanent and temporary exhibitions revealing the history of the capital from prehistoric times to the present day. The ever-changing displays might cover anything from photographs of football fans to displays about royal fashion. Star exhibits include the spectacular gilded Lord Mayor's coach (wheeled out once a year for the eponymous Show – see also) to a genuine c18 prison cell complete with prisoners' graffiti. At lunchtimes there are also occasional free lectures and films. / Times: 4.30pm-5.30pm; www.museumoflondon.org.uk; Tube: Barbican, Bank, St Paul's, Moorgate; café.

Museum of St Bartholomew's Hospital EC1

West Smithfield   (020) 7601 8152   5–2B

Original archives, artefacts and medical instruments, together with video and sound recordings, tell the story of this famous hospital from its foundation in 1123 to the present day. Of particular interest is the Charter signed by Henry VIII preventing the closure of the hospital during the Dissolution of the Monasteries and eight new sound recordings of doctors and nurses recreating their daily lives from 1500-present. Kids might particularly like the amputation kits and bleeding bowls, and the wooden head used for practising trepanning (drilling through the scalp). / Times: Tue-Fri 10am-4pm; Tube: Barbican, St Paul's.

Museum of the Honorable Artillery Company EC1

Armoury House, City Rd
(020) 7382 1533, (020) 7382 1537   5–1C

The Honorable Artillery Company was founded in 1537 by Henry VIII from the existing Guild of St George. It was directed to "attend to the better defence of the Realm" and encouraged exercise in handling bows and handguns. The museum was set up in 1987 to commemorate the Company's 450th anniversary. Highlights include uniforms, Chinese porcelain with the HAC coat of arms, and swords. Donations are appreciated. / Times: visits & tours by telephone appt; Tube: Moorgate, Liverpool Street, Old Street.

Museums of the Royal College of Surgeons of England WC2
35-43 Lincoln's Inn Fields   (020) 7405 3474   5–2A
The College has four collections: the Hunterian Museum and the Odontological Museum, and the Wellcome Museums of Pathology and Anatomy. The Hunterian Museum has paintings by George Stubbs, the 7'10" skeleton of Charles O'Brien (the Irish giant) and c18 surgical instruments. Donations are encouraged and children under 14 must be accompanied. Check with the visitors co-ordinator before setting out.
/ Times: Hunterian & Odontological Museums Mon-Fri 10am-5pm; Wellcome Museums Mon-Fri 9am-5pm by appt; www.rcseng.ac.uk; Tube: Holborn, Temple.

Oak Room EC1
173 Rosebery Ave
(020) 7833 9527 and ask for the concierge   4–3D
On four days a year (ring for details), and only by prior appointment, this 17th century room, designed by Wren's protégé Grinling Gibbons, is open to the public. It was built originally as the boardroom (in modern parlance) of the New River Company (an important early scheme to bring clean water to the metropolis), and has been moved from its initial location. / Tube: Angel (or 19 or 38 buses).

Old Bailey EC4
Newgate St   (020) 7248 3277   5–2B
The Central Criminal Court, as it is more properly called, is the site of London's most notorious trials. All human life is there, and there's usually something intriguing, amusing or just plain bizarre to listen to. If you're only paying a brief visit, the most interesting thing to do is to catch the cross-examination of a witness by a bewigged barrister. There are two public gallery entrances: Warwick Passage, off Old Bailey, and Newgate Street. Children below the age of 14 are not allowed.
/ Times: Mon-Fri 10.30am-1pm, 2pm-4pm; Tube: St Paul's, Blackfriars.

Prince Henry's Room EC4
17 Fleet St   (020) 7936 2710   5–2A
In one of the few buildings in the City to survive the Great Fire, this small room retains its original panelling and plaster work. The naming of the building is honorific only (referring to the eldest son of James I) and it now houses a selection of memorabilia of diarist Samuel Pepys. The curators are enthusiasts for the great man and are pleased to share their knowledge. / Times: 11am-2pm, closed Sun & bank hol weekends; Tube: Temple.

Royal Mail Mount Pleasant Sorting Office EC1
Farringdon Rd   (020) 7239 2311   5–1A
If you've always wondered how the mail gets distributed, a visit here should answer your questions. There are two tours, at 2pm and 2.30pm (Mon-Thu). They cover the sorting office, the mechanical sorting equipment and the Mail Rail – the unstaffed underground railway which distributes post around the capital. To arrange a visit call to book – individuals are welcome. You will have to confirm in writing two weeks before you go. Children under nine are not admitted. / Times: Mon-Thu 2pm & 2.30pm by appt; Tube: Farringdon, King's Cross, Chancery Lane.

St John Ambulance Exhibition EC1
Priory House, St John's Ln   (020) 7253 6644   5–1A
Opposite St John's Gate (see also), this museum houses items from the formation of the St John Ambulance Association in 1887. The exhibition, Time to Care, showcases stories of St John Ambulance work and includes training equipment, models, photographs and displays illustrating the activities of the association in times of war. / Times: Mon-Sat 10am-5pm (Sat 4pm); www.sja.org.uk; Tube: Farringdon.

Saint John's Gate EC1
St John's Lane   (020) 7253 6644   5–1A
Built in 1504, the Gate was the entrance to the English HQ of the crusading Knights Hospitallers and has been variously a coffee house (run by Richard Hogarth, father of painter William) and a tavern. It is now the base of the British Order of St John, and home to the Museum and Library of the Order of St John (see also). Tours take in parts of the building (including the museum) not usually open to the public. These areas include the c14 Grand Priory Church and the c12 Crypt (one of London's few remaining Norman buildings). Donations are appreciated. / Times: Mon-Sat 10am-5pm (Sat 4pm); tours Tue, Fri & Sat 11am & 2.30pm; if group of 10+ please call ahead; www.sja.org.uk; Tube: Farringdon, Barbican.

Salvation Army International Heritage Centre EC4
101 Queen Victoria St   (020) 7332 0101   5–3A
Discover the history of the Salvation Army and why its founder, William Booth, devoted his life to the poor and homeless. The exhibition is located at the Salvation Army's International headquarters. A 50 minute recorded tour of the exhibition is available at no charge. Call for further information. / Times: Mon-Fri 9.30am-3.30pm; www.salvationarmy.org; Tube: Mansion House, Black Friars.

Wesley's Chapel EC1

49 City Rd   (020) 7253 2262   5–1C

John Wesley, the father of Methodism, had his chapel and house built in 1778 to the designs of George Dance the Younger. You can visit the chapel and Wesley's tomb, which are part of this fine group of Georgian buildings on the northern fringe of the City. (Wesley's House and the Museum of Methodism can also be visited during the same hours, but for these there is a charge.) / Times: Mon-Sat 10am-4pm, Sun 12pm-2pm; Tube: Old Street, Moorgate.

Outdoor attractions

Broadgate* EC2

(020) 7505 4000   5–2D

One summer (end May-beginning of Sep) lunchtime, when the weather is hot, why not visit the City's Broadgate development. Most weekdays between 12.30pm and 2pm, this Manhattan-style complex of offices, shops and restaurants puts on musical or other entertainments (usually at some point including an unusual exhibition, in the past it has been a display of Spanish dressage with Andalucian horses). Giant chess and draughts sets are provided, too. During the winter, you could spend an evening (dress warmly) watching teams compete at broomball on Britain's only permanent outdoor ice-rink – or try ice-skating for yourself (there is a charge). A monthly diary of events – Broadgate Live – is available from the Arena office (or you can call to be put on the mailing list). / Tube: Liverpool Street.

Inns of Court

(020) 7427 4800 (Middle Temple);
(020) 7405 1393 (Lincoln's Inn);
(020) 7458 7800 (Gray's Inn)   5–2A

Lawyers have clustered around the City since the earliest times. Even today, every barrister practising in England and Wales must be a member of one of the four inns of court (the Middle and Inner Temples, Gray's and Lincoln's Inns). These bodies are effectively medieval colleges, with their own dining halls, libraries, gardens and chapels. They are also landlords to the barristers' 'chambers' (or offices).

All of the inns give the public access to some part of their territories, which are peaceful, charming and often of considerable antiquity.

Starting in the Temple, don't miss Middle Temple Hall, a large Tudor hall with a magnificent double hammer-beam roof. This area is also rich in historical trivia – not only was Twelfth Night first performed in the hall here by the Bard's own company, but the Wars of the Roses took their name from red and white blooms plucked from the garden behind. The hall at the neighbouring Inner Temple is not open to the public, but the main sight there is the Temple Church, the only circular church in London and one of London's oldest buildings (c12).

Leaving the Temple, and progressing up Chancery Lane, you come first to Lincoln's Inn, with its fine, sweeping lawns, halls (one c15, one c19) and library, and then to Gray's Inn, whose chapel and walks are open to public view. Organised groups can see the inside of the rest of the building, including the medieval hall, by writing to the Under Treasurer, Honorable Society of Gray's Inn, Treasury Office, 8 South Square, London WC1R 5EU.

The grounds of all the inns are open on weekdays. Mid-morning and mid-afternoons of weekdays are generally the best times to gain access to the halls and chapels – if you are making a special trip, it may be wise to call to confirm access. / Times: Middle Temple 10am–11.30am, 2pm–4pm; Lincoln's Inn 7am–7pm; Gray's Inn (call for times); Tube: Temple, Chancery Lane.

The Monument* EC2
Monument St & Fish St Hill   5–3C
The Great Fire of 1666 swept away much of the medieval City. The burghers of the day commissioned Wren to memorialise the devastation and the Monument – still the highest free-standing stone column in the world – was the result. Its height (202 feet) is the same as its distance from the baker's shop in Pudding Lane where the fire started. The story is given in detail in the large notice at the base of the column. You can climb to the top, but there's a small charge. / Tube: Monument.

Postman's Park EC1
Little Britain, King Edward St   5–2B
A tiny entrance opposite the National Postal Museum leads into a small and unprepossessing park with benches and grass. However, follow the path and you see a long wooden porch protecting what looks like the rear wall of a block of flats and a slightly raised patio. Set into the wall are around 50 memorials to 'heroic men and women', many with a story to tell, and on the south side of the park is Michel Ayrton's bronze Minotaur, added in 1973. / Tube: St Paul's, Barbican.

Riverside Walk
See the introduction of the South section for suggestions of interesting walks by the Thames.

Tower Bridge* SE I

(020) 7403 3761
24-hour Bridge Lift information line (020) 7378 7700
5–4D

One of London's great symbols, the bridge was built between 1886 and 1894. Despite its appearance, it is, in fact, a thoroughly modern steel structure, but was clad in stone to harmonise with the Tower of London. The halves of the bridge (which was originally steam-powered, but is now electrically operated) can still be raised to accommodate large vessels needing access to the Pool of London – ring the number given to find out when the bridge is next scheduled to be raised. There is a fascinating display inside the bridge, but at quite a significant charge. / www.towerbridge.org.uk; Tube: Tower Hill.

Tower of London* EC3

West Gate, Tower of London   (020) 7709 0765   5–3D

The Tower of London is one of the most interesting and historic sites in London and unfortunately charges handsomely for entering its precincts or visiting the treasures within (which, of course, include the Crown Jewels). You can get a good perspective of the medieval building from the riverside walk, however (and see also Ceremony of the Keys).
/ www.tower-of-london.com; Tube: Tower Hill.

East London

Introduction

Centuries of being the poor relation among the areas of London has left east London ('the East End') with a very different range of amenities from any other area. It means for example that in the inner city there is only one park of any note, **Victoria Park**. However, if you are prepared to go as far as the end of the Central Line, you will, in **Epping Forest**, find the largest medieval woodland anywhere near London. A feature of east London (and much less common elsewhere) which is of particular interest to children, is the city farms.

As regeneration of the 'East End proper' takes hold, however, some very notable attractions are springing up. **Canary Wharf**, the largest office development in Europe, has given the Isle of Dogs Britain's tallest building, at 50 storeys high. The redevelopment of **St Katharine's Dock** has created what is by far the nicest marina in inner London – on a sunny day, it's a really charming place. The continuing efforts to improve the **Lee Valley** are beginning to make it an amenity which offers a large range of attractions.

The area is well served with non-commercial art galleries (the **Whitechapel Gallery** being the grandest and longest established).

For people-watching and browsing, the area has several of the most characterful markets in London – **Petticoat Lane** and **Brick Lane**, and **Columbia Road Flower Market**, which are particularly popular Sunday morning destinations, and can be joined together on an interesting stroll (especially if you take in the former Truman Brewery on Brick Lane, which has been funkily redeveloped into a series of retail and gallery spaces with cafés and bars).

A trip on the (overground) Docklands Light Railway (from Bank or Tower Hill; www.dlr.co.uk) is an ideal way to see the much of the area. Travel is free if you have a Travelcard and, at weekends, a running commentary points out all the old dock areas and London's original Chinatown at Limehouse. End your trip in Greenwich and explore (see South London).

Essex Tourist Information Centre, Essex
County Hall, Market Rd, Chelmsford   (01245) 283400
/ *Times: Mon-Sat 10am-5pm (Sat 4pm); www.essexcc.gov.uk; BR: Chelmsford.*

Redbridge Tourist Information Centre, Essex
Clements Rd, Ilford   (020) 8478 3020, (020) 8478 7145
/ *Times: Mon-Sat 9.30am-8pm (Sat 4pm); www.redbridge.gov.uk; BR: Ilford.*

Thurrock Tourist Centre, Essex
Granada Motorway Service Area (M25),
Thurrock (01708) 863733
*/ Times: summer 9am-5pm (Sat & Sun 3pm); winter Mon-Fri 9am-4.30pm,
Sat 9.30am-3pm, Sun 9.30am-12.30pm; www.thurrock-community.org.uk;
BR: Grays.*

Tower Hamlets Tourist Information Centre E1
18 Lamb St (020) 7375 2539
*The information centre at Liverpool Street Station will also be
useful for visitors to the markets (see The City). / Times: Mon-Fri
9.30am-1.30pm & 2pm-14.30pm (closed Wed pm & Sat); Sun
11.30am-2.30pm; Tube: Liverpool Street.*

Indoor attractions

Association of Photographers Gallery EC2
81 Leonard St (020) 7739 3631 5–1C
*A contemporary photographic gallery, holding ten to twelve
temporary exhibitions annually. / Times: Mon-Fri 9.30am-6pm, Sat
12pm-4pm; www.aophoto.co.uk; Tube: Old Street.*

Bethnal Green Museum of Childhood E2
Cambridge Heath Rd (020) 8983 5200 1–2D
*Housing the V&A's collection of toys, games, puppets, dolls and
dolls houses (of which there are over 40), this repository of
children's memorabilia offers quite enough to interest children
and parents. There are workshops for children on most
Saturdays, and school holiday activities. The museum has
an excellent supply of free literature about London attractions,
particularly those in the East End. / Times: Mon-Thu, Sat-Sun
10am-5.50pm; www.vam.ac.uk/vastatic/nmc; Tube: Bethnal Green; café.*

Brooking Collection, Kent
University of Greenwich (Dartford Campus),
Oakfield Ln (020) 8331 9897
*Windows rescued from Windsor, doorknobs from 10 Downing
Street ..., this unique and comprehensive collection, amassed
by Charles Brooking over 35 years, contains over 100,000
architectural details from the past five centuries includes doors,
staircase sections, bootscrapers and rainwater heads. Many
visitors to the collection come because they inhabit a period
property which they want to restore or refurbish and want a
point of reference. Information on more than 7,000 items is
held on computer and examples of details of specific types or
particular periods can be retrieved prior to the visit. / Times: by
appt, 9am-5pm (also weekends & evenings for groups); BR: Dartford (then 476
bus).*

Chisenhale Gallery E3
64 Chisenhale Rd (020) 8981 4518 1–2D
*This contemporary gallery holds half a dozen mixed media
shows a year by British and foreign artists. Many of the British
artists shown here have subsequently been nominated for the
prestigious Turner Prize. / Times: Wed-Sun 1pm-6pm;
www.chisenhale.org.uk; Tube: Mile End, Bethnal Green.*

Clowns Gallery E8

1 Hillman St   (020) 7608 0312 (office hours only)   1–1D
As the name suggests, you will find all sorts of artefacts and
archive material relating to clowns at this museum/gallery
opposite Hackney Town Hall. Parents beware! There is also
a joke shop in which kids will want to spend their pocket
money. The evening of the first Tue in the month is a 'social'
with speakers and films, for example, on subjects of clownish
interest – donations greatly appreciated. / Times: 1st Tue of month
6.30pm-10.30pm, 1st Fri of month 12pm-5pm; other times by arrangement
including groups of up to 50 (Note: For large groups, there will be a small
charge.); www.clowns-international.co.uk; BR: Hackney Central, Hackney
Downs.

Geffrye Museum E2

Kingsland Rd   (020) 7739 9893   1–2D
This is a rather special museum, situated in elegant early c18
almshouses, which tells the story of English domestic interiors
through a series of period rooms from Elizabethan times to
the 1990s. There's also an enchanting walled herb garden
and a fine display of period gardens, showing a visual history
of town gardens over the past four hundred years. In summer
the museum organises unusual, intelligent activities for kids and
there is often music (not always period), inside or in the garden
– ask for a programme. Most Londoners will never have been
here – they should go. / Times: Tue-Sat 10am-5pm, Sun & bank hols
12pm-5pm; www.geffrye-museum.org.uk; Tube: Liverpool Street, Old Street;
café.

Hackney Museum E8

Mare St   (020) 8986 6914   1–1D
The museum is in the process of moving just across the road
to the Technology and Learning Centre that is currently being
built, and so is closed until Spring 2002. It will still celebrate
the history of Hackney from Viking times in a programme
of changing exhibitions, just with a facelift and lots of new
computer and IT exhibitions, as well as hands-on activities.
It's the displays that reflect the area's cultural diversity which
are the particular attraction. Perhaps of special interest to
local residents is 'Hackney Voices', a CD-ROM of information,
photographs and interviews with first-generation Hackney
residents about their experiences of settling the borough.
/ Times: Mon-Sat 10am-5pm; www.hackney.gov.uk/hackneymuseum;
BR: Hackney Central.

Hazel Ceramics Workshop*

Stallion's Yard, Codham Hall, Great Warley,
near Brentwood   (01277) 220892
See how an award-winning range of collectable ceramic wall
plaques is made. (If you decide you want to participate, there's
a small charge.) / Times: Fri-Sun & bank hol Mon 11am-5pm;
www.hazle.com; BR: Brentwood (then 265 bus).

London Ambulance Service Museum, Essex
North Division HQ, Aldborough Rd South, Ilford
(020) 8557 1767
It includes more than 20 vehicles – ranging from the horse-drawn ambulance of 1870 to a paramedic motorcycle of 1991 – but the museum also places much emphasis on the human aspects of the ambulance service. Curiosities include a first aid box that belonged to Prince Albert. / Times: by appt Mon-Fri 9.30am-4pm; www.lond-amb.sthames.nhs.uk; Tube: Newbury Park.

London Chest Hospital E2
3rd Floor, Bonner Rd, Victoria Park
(020) 8983 2212   1–2D
The Capel Collection consists of 25 instruments and books of/on instruments relating to chest medicine collected since the Hospital was founded in 1848. There is a larger, more general collection at Royal London Hospital (see also). / Times: by appt; Tube: Bethnal Green or D3 bus.

Manor Park Museum E12
Romford Rd, Manor Park   (020) 8514 0274
The museum has been moved around the borough in recent times and is now in the old reading room of the Manor Park library. It offers local history displays (geared towards schools' requirements), as well as temporary exhibitions. / Times: Tue, Fri & Sat 10am-5pm, Thu 1pm-8pm; www.newham.gov.uk/leisure/museums; BR: Manor Park.

Matt's Gallery E3
42-44 Copperfield Rd   (020) 8983 1771   1–2D
This contemporary gallery commissions works ranging from installations which are made in – and specifically for – the space, to video, photography and painting exhibitions. Call for details of exhibitions. / Times: Wed-Sun 12pm-6pm (exhibitions); Tube: Mile End.

Forest & Co E15
Lancaster House, Lancaster Rd, Leytonstone
(020) 8556 7009   1–2D
Go to this official auctioneers for HM Customs and Excise (also private vendors and bailiffs) to listen to the patter. Sales include everything from cars through carpets, jewellery, bric-à-brac and antiques. / Times: Thu, from 11am; Tube: Leytonstone.

North Woolwich Old Station Museum E16
Pier Rd, North Woolwich   (020) 7474 7244
This restored Victorian station, now a museum, tells the story of the local railways of east London and their impact on the areas they served. There are tickets, timetables, posters, a reconstructed '20s ticket office and, of course, trains. The first Sun of every month (Easter-Oct) is a steam day, on which a locomotive raises steam and moves around a short track. Occasionally, there are film shows and model railway days. There are kids events during school holidays – book places in advance. / Times: Sat & Sun 1pm-5pm; school hols Mon-Sun 1pm-5pm (free activities for kids); www.newham.gov.uk/leisure/museums/moldstn.htm; Tube: East Ham (then 101 bus), Stratford (then 69 bus), North Woolwich.

Plashet Zoo E7

Plashet Park, Shrewsbury Rd   (020) 8503 5994

If you would like to see animals more exotic than you would normally find in a city farm, why not visit the collection here – all year round, you can laugh at the llamas, wave at the wallabies, ogle the owls and gawp at the goats. Some of the favourite animals include Dandy, the free wandering turkey, Kookaburra, a bird that laughs back at you, and Joe the Pony, a recent addition. In summer you can see tropical butterflies emerging and falconry displays. Other reasons to visit include the Pheasant Garden. Donations are encouraged. / Times: summer Tue-Sun 10am-5pm; winter Tue-Sun 10am-4pm; Tube: East Ham; café.

Ragged School Museum E3

46-50 Copperfield Rd   (020) 8980 6405   1–2D

This museum of the history of the East End is housed in a Victorian canalside warehouse which, from 1895, formed part of the largest ragged (free) school in London. Appropriately, education and the life and work of Dr Barnardo are given particular emphasis, and there is a recreated Victorian classroom (which is used by school groups for re-enacted Victorian lessons). On the first Sun of the month there are family arts and crafts workshops. During the school holidays, activities are organised, from making Victorian sweets to treasure hunts. All are popular and space is limited – call for a free programme. / Times: Wed & Thu 9am-5pm, 1st Sun of month 2pm-5pm; www.raggedschoolmuseum.org.uk; Tube: Mile End; café.

Royal London Hospital Archives E1

St Augustine with St Philip's Church, Newark St
(020) 7377 7608   1–2D

The permanent exhibition about the history of the famous hospital is housed in the basement of a c19 church. Highlights include a small Hogarth drawing, George Washington's false teeth, nursing uniforms from the 1900s, documents relating to Elephant Man Joseph Merrick (and a copy of his hat) and a bust of and watercolours by WWI heroine Edith Cavell (who trained here), as well as her last letters to her nurses from her condemned cell and the flag that covered her coffin. There are also videos, including films from the 1930s showing what it was like being a nurse and a patient then. / Times: Mon-Fri 10am-4.30pm (occasionally closed 1pm-2pm); Tube: Whitechapel.

The Showroom E2

44 Bonner Rd   (020) 8983 4115   1–2D

As at the other two galleries nearby (Matt's and the Chisenhale), the contemporary works displayed here are often installation-based, but may include performance art and videos. There are four exhibitions per year, lasting five weeks each. Call for exhibition information. / Times: Wed-Sun 1pm-6pm (exhibitions); www.theshowroom.org; Tube: Bethnal Green.

Spitalfields Market E1
Brushfield St   (020) 7247 8556   5–2D
*The City's former fruit and vegetable market (vacated in 1991)
is now run by the same company as Camden Lock. It has been
transformed into a mixed development that is a particularly
popular Sunday destination. The heart of the market is the
stalls selling arts and crafts, bric-à-brac, the latest fashions
and organic food. Spitalfields makes a great lunch stop as there
is an International Food Village, (with offerings from Mexican
chilli to Turkish kebabs). Regular special events include an
alternative fashion week, a dog show, a community festival
and a harvest festival. / Times: Mon-Fri 10am-6pm, Sun 10am-5.30pm;
Tube: Liverpool Street.*

Thames Police Museum E1
Marine Support Unit, 98 Wapping High St
(020) 7275 4421   1–3D
*This collection documents the history of the Marine Police;
artefacts date from 1798 – the date of the first organised
London police force. Weapons, including cutlasses, model boats
and uniforms, are all displayed in a pleasant setting overlooking
the Thames. / Times: by written appt, groups & clubs preferred;
Tube: Wapping.*

Thurrock Museum, Essex
Thameside Complex, Orsett Road, Grays
(01375) 382555
*A permanent gallery of the history of the Thurrock area,
displaying archaeology from the Stone Age to the medieval
period. / Times: Mon-Sat 9am-5pm; www.thurrock.gov.uk/museum;
BR: Grays.*

Upminster Tithe Barn
Agricultural & Folk Museum, Essex
Hall Lane, Upminster   (01708) 457266
*The barn is a large thatched, timber-framed structure, probably
built around 1420. It contains a collection illustrating the
farming, urban and social history of the community and shows
the transition of the area from countryside to suburbia. There
are over 13,000 exhibits, including old agricultural implements,
farriers' tools, dairying equipment, bicycles, photographs,
laundry paraphernalia (from the time when it was all done
manually) and toys and games. / Times: 1st full weekend of each
month Apr-Oct inclusive & Heritage Weekend in Sept, 2pm-5.30pm;
www.upminster.com/upminster/history/tithe.htm; BR: Upminster (then 248 bus);
light refreshment stand.*

Upminster Windmill, Essex

St Mary's Lane, Upminster   (01708) 457266

This white five-storey smock mill was built in the early c19 and worked commercially until around 1935. It is owned by the London Borough of Havering and staffed by members of Hornchurch & District Historical Society. The mill has undergone substantial repair, and it is hoped to have it working again in due course. / Times: Apr-Sep, 3rd Sat & Sun of month, 2pm-5pm & National Mills Day (2nd Sun of May instead of 3rd weekend that month); www.upminster.com/upminster/history/windmill.htm; BR: Upminster Station; Tube: Upminster.

Valence House Museum, Essex

Becontree Ave, Dagenham   (020) 8595 8404

This partly moated, c17 manor house, contains various locally discovered artefacts dating from the Stone Age onwards. Its most notable contents, perhaps, are fine portraits of the Fanshawe family, including some by Lely and Kneller. There are also domestic interiors from the c17 and c20, displays on the history of Dagenham Village and a walled herb garden. Children's workshops are held periodically. / Times: Tue-Fri 9.30am-1pm & 2pm-4.30pm, Sat 10am-4pm; www.bardaglea.org.uk/4-valence/valence-menu.html; BR: Chadwell Heath; Tube: Becontree; café Sat only.

Vestry House Museum E17

Vestry Rd, Walthamstow   (020) 8509 1917

This prettily-situated workhouse (1730) was converted into a museum of local history in the 1930s. It is in the old village of Walthamstow (which is worth a visit in its own right). The most singular exhibit is probably the Bremer Car, which is claimed to be one of the first petrol-driven cars to be made in London. An original police cell (used between 1840 and 1870) is another curiosity. There is a programme of temporary exhibitions. / Times: Mon-Fri 10am-1pm, 2pm-5.15pm (Sat 5pm), closed bank hols; Tube: Walthamstow Central.

Void Gallery E2

511 Hackney Rd   (020) 7729 9976   1–2D

A gallery exhibiting both local and international artists in a diverse range of media with a focus on contemporary art, with the intent to "produce and facilitate innovative exhibitions that contribute to current debates in contemporary arts discourse". / Times: Fri-Sun 12pm-6pm, but call first; www.voidgallery.com; Tube: Bethnal Green.

Waltham Abbey Church, Essex

Highbridge Street, Waltham Abbey   (01992) 767897

King Harold is said to be buried beneath this Norman abbey, which was rebuilt in 1120. The crypt centre contains shows an exhibition about the history of the town and abbey, which is close to Lee Valley Park (see also). / Times: 10am (12pm on Sun & 11am on Wed)-6pm (4pm in winter); BR: Waltham Cross Station.

Whitechapel Art Gallery E1

80 Whitechapel High St (020) 7522 7888,
recorded information (020) 7522 7878 5–2D
This important non-commercial venue, in its atmospheric Art Nouveau building, has no permanent collection. It can therefore make a virtue of necessity, presenting an ever-changing series of exhibitions of c20 and contemporary art, often of important and challenging artists. For details ring the recorded information line. There is generally a programme of talks around the exhibitions, and sometimes also early-evening films.
/ Times: Tue-Sun 11am-5pm (Wed 8pm); www.whitechapel.org;
Tube: Aldgate East; café.

William Morris Gallery E17

Lloyd Park, Forest Rd (020) 8527 3782
William Morris, born in Walthamstow in 1834, was probably the most influential designer and craftsman London has ever produced. He died in 1896, but his ideas were carried on by the Arts and Crafts movement into the 1920s, and many of his designs, especially for wallpaper, are still in production today. This delightful c18 house in its own grounds contains a display of Morris's work and personal memorabilia, together with examples of the products of his associates, Burne-Jones, Rossetti and Philip Webb. / Times: Tue-Sat & 1st Sun of month 10am-1pm & 2pm-5pm; www.lbwf.gov.uk/wmg; Tube: Walthamstow Central.

Outdoor attractions

BBC Essex Garden, Essex

Crowther Nurseries, Ongar Rd, Abridge (01708) 688581
The garden in which Ken Crowther tries out new products and techniques for the benefit of fans of his Saturday BBC radio show, 'Down to Earth', a garden magazine programme. Consisting of a vegetable plot, two small greenhouses, herbaceous and shrub border, and new shrub rose beds in the works for 2001, this garden is open to visitors even during filming for the show. If you time your visit accordingly, you may ask a question to which the answer may subsequently be broadcast. / Times: 9am-5.30pm; BR: Theydon Bois (then 500 bus); café.

Brick Lane Market E1

1–2D
Forget the papers – roll up early in the morning to start off Sunday with a truly East End 'pile it high, sell it cheap' experience. 'It' might be almost anything. / Times: Sun 6am-1pm;
Tube: Aldgate, Aldgate East, Liverpool Street, Shoreditch; café.

Canary Wharf E14

(020) 7418 2783 (box office/events information) 1–3D
*Cesar Pelli's great tower (244m high) on the Isle of Dogs is,
at 50 storeys, the tallest building in Britain. You don't need
to approach it to appreciate it – you can see it from all over
London – but if you do, there's an impressive shopping mall at
its base with more than 60 shops and restaurants. There are
many other shiny, new buildings around the tower's base, which
are worth a view – over 5 million square feet of office and
retail space has been created and occupied in the area since
1991. The public spaces are well-kept and provide many
different views of the tower: look for the fountain in Cabot
Square, which is controlled by a computer that changes the
water level if it's windy to stop people getting sprayed. There
is a regular programme of arts and events, many of which are
free, including outside events in the summer. The twin towers
that now flank Pelli's behemoth were completed in 2001.*
/ www.canarywharf.com; Tube: Canary Wharf (DLR).

Columbia Road Flower Market E2

Columbia Rd 5–1D
*Every Sunday morning this east London street (with a few
neighbouring alleys) bursts into bloom – you'll know you are
near the market when you see the occasional palm tree
walking through the streets, possibly in the company of shrubs
and boxes of herbs. It's best to arrive early – it all gets terribly
crowded. A trip here combines well with a visit to Spitalfields
Market and Brick Lane.* / Times: Sun 8am-12.30pm; Tube: Old Street,
Liverpool Street, Shoreditch.

East Ham Nature Reserve E6

Norman Rd (020) 8470 4525
*The two suburban nature trails here have the mission of
introducing everyone to the joys of nature. Set in London's
largest churchyard (in use since Norman times, though the
oldest stones date from the c17), the trails are fully accessible
(including to people in wheelchairs). A highly informative,
illustrated guide is available from the Visitor Centre – a Braille
version is also available. Ring to ensure the reserve is open
before you set off.* / Times: Tue-Fri 10am-5pm, Sat & Sun 2pm-5pm
(winter 1pm-4pm); Tube: East Ham.

Epping Forest, Essex
(020) 8508 0028
Two miles by 12, this ancient forest on the eastern fringe of London (owned by the Corporation of London since Victorian times) is the largest public open space in Essex. Great effort is put into maintaining the landscape, with its diverse natural history, and the area is designated as a Site of Special Scientific Interest. Although the forest is a very popular destination, it's big enough that you can lose yourself in it – real countryside AND accessible from a tube station! A particular attraction is Queen Elizabeth's Hunting Lodge (small charge to visit), near Chingford, which is the only surviving Tudor 'hunt-standing' (from which the monarch could view the hunt's progress). The information centre at High Beech organises occasional walks through the forest (details from the number given). At this spot (it's around two miles from Loughton), there is an easy-access path and also tracks that are popular with horse riders and mountain bikers. / Times: information centre, summer, 10am (Sun 11am)-5pm; winter, Mon-Fri 11am-3pm, Sat &Sun 10am (Sun 11am)-dusk; www.cityoflondon.gov.uk; Tube: Epping, Theydon Bois, Loughton, Snaresbrook, Debden.

Flitch Way
(01376) 340262
The Flitch Way is a country park passing through 15 miles of countryside along the former Bishop's Stortford to Braintree railway line. Your journey passes wildlife-rich railway cuttings, Victorian stations, farmland, villages and woodland. The Centre has an exhibition room of local history, open on Sundays. / Times: centre-Mon-Sat 8am-5pm, Sun 1pm-4pm; BR: Braintree.

The Greenway
(020) 8472 1430 (ask for Park & Leisure Services)
Formerly less romantically described as the Northern Outfall Sewer Embankment, this elevated feature of the landscape was built in the 1860s to provide a sewage and drainage system for east London. Shedding its original image, the four mile long (and then beyond into Hackney) path now has been developed as a wildlife habitat and provides unfettered open spaces for walkers and cyclists. The route begins from Royal Dock Road in E6, and runs to Stratford High Road in E15 and beyond into Hackney. Along the entire route, there are access points for visitors and noticeboards about native flora and fauna. / Tube: Beckton (DLR), West Ham.

Greenwich Foot Tunnel E14

(020) 8854 8888 ext 5493 (to confirm lift times)   1–3D

The tunnel, opened in 1902, connects Greenwich with the Isle of Dogs and was built because the steamboat ferry was contributing to excessive congestion of the river at this point. It lies 10 metres below the low water mark, is 390m long and is made of cast iron segments, lined with concrete and tiled. New lifts were installed in 1992, replacing equipment which had lasted since 1904. After 1999, when the Jubilee Line opened between Greenwich and Canary Wharf, the practical function of the tunnel was somewhat overshadowed, although the appeal of walking under the Thames continues to attract children of all ages. / Times: lift service, Mon-Sat 7am-7pm, Sun 10am-5.30pm; tunnel 24 hours; www.greenwich.gov.uk; Tube: Greenwich, Island Gardens (DLR).

Hackney City Farm E2

1a Goldsmith's Row   (020) 7729 6381   1–2D

Hackney City Farm keeps as full a range as possible of traditional farm livestock in its one and a half-acre site. It also boasts a prize-winning herd of pedigree saddleback pigs. In spring, the lambs and calves are a particular reason to take the children. (On Thursdays and Sundays, pottery making is offered at a rate of 50p an hour.) / Times: Tue-Sun 10am-4.30pm (& bank hols); www.members.nbci.com; Tube: Bethnal Green; BR: Hackney; café.

Hainault Forest Country Park, Essex

(020) 8500 7353

This square mile of woodland was dedicated to the public in 1906 and is one of the few remaining vestiges of the great forest of Essex and Waltham (see also Epping Forest). It is a Site of Special Scientific Interest because of the ancient woodland, pollarded trees and flora and fauna. Foxburrows Farm conserves rare breeds and employs traditional farm practices. Activities in the summer events programme might include a storytelling picnic, a fungi-finding expedition, orienteering and a bat search. In the winter, there are bird-feeding days and Christmas decorations workshops. / Times: 7am-dusk; Tube: Hainault then 247 or 362 bus (or BR to Romford or Ilford then 150 or 247 bus); café.

Hainault Lodge Nature Reserve, Essex

(020) 8500 7353 (Hainault Country Park)

Redbridge Borough's first Local Nature Reserve is remarkable for its views across London and for the variety of habitats within its small area. You need to obtain permission and arrange an appointment (from Pam and Tony Simpson (020) 8599 7818) to enter the 14-acre site (adjacent to the park), but everyone is welcome and tours can be arranged. Creatures you might see include many nesting birds and small mammals – if you are very lucky you might spot the rare Black Rabbit. / Tube: Hainault then 247 or 362 bus (or BR to Romford or Ilford then 150 or 247 bus).

Hatfield Forest, Herts

Estate Office, Takeley, Bishop's Stortford   (01279) 870678

A rare surviving example of a medieval royal hunting forest, it is a Site of Special Scientific Interest and a national nature reserve. The forest comprises over 400 hectares of ancient coppice woodland with two ornamental lakes, the c18 Shell House, a stream and a marsh reserve. / Times: Easter-Oct 31 10am-5pm; November-Easter-weekends & school holidays 11am-3pm; BR: Bishop's Stortford.

Island History Trust E14

Docklands Settlement, 197 East Ferry Rd
(020) 7987 6041   1–3D

The Trust documents the social history of the Isle of Dogs, which has seen massive industrial growth, severe bomb damage, recession and most recently large-scale urban renewal. Five thousand pictures – from the 1870s to the 1960s – show street scenes, churches, sport, work, social lives, pubs and families. All are captioned and indexed and so of particular interest to people who have a connection with the area, or who wish to research family history. The area is named for a small island in the Thames which has long since disappeared – the site was never itself an island. / Times: Tue, Wed, and 1st Sun of every month 1.30pm-4.30pm; www.islandhistory.org.uk; Tube: Island Gardens (DLR), Mudchute (DLR).

Lee Valley Park, Essex

Enquiries to: Countryside Centre, Abbey Gardens,
Waltham Abbey, Essex EN9 1XQ   (01992) 713838

Since 1967, the derelict valley of the River Lee has been being transformed into over 1,000 acres of 'green chain', extending out from Hackney, via Tottenham and Enfield, to the more truly rural delights of Hertfordshire and Essex. You can walk the whole 23 miles on the towpath, or cycle it – it is part of the National Cycle Network linking Hertfordshire with Harwich. Natural attractions include a variety of bird life and a dragonfly sanctuary. Man-made items of interest include some pretty and historic c18 buildings, among them the largest restored tidal mill left standing in Britain (open Sun, 2pm-4pm, small charge, (020) 8215 0050) and the Clock Mill. Within the park, you can also find Lee Valley Walk, a 50-mile regional walking trail from London to Luton, and River Lee Country Park, where you might be lucky enough to spot the rare bittern or smew (bird hides are open to all on weekends). If you're planning a visit, contact the Countryside Centre to pick up relevant leaflets. All parts of the Park are easily accessible from the rail line which runs alongside. / Times: centre, April-Oct, 9.30am-5pm; Nov-Feb, Tue-Sun 10am-4.30pm; www.leevalleypark.org.uk; Tube: Tottenham Hale.

Mudchute Park & Farm E14

Pier St   (020) 7515 5901   1–3D

The largest urban farm in London, this 32-acre site is the most significant open space on the Isle of Dogs. It includes a riding arena, fields, a wild section, a picnic area and thousands of recently planted trees. Because it's several times bigger than most of the other farms, it can be run largely as if it were a small farm in the country – complete with its own grassland for grazing. On the livestock front, the speciality here is sheep, of which a wide variety are kept, but there are also cattle, goats and pigs. Each year there is a family day in July. / Times: summer 9am-5pm; winter 10am-4.30pm; Tube: Crossharbour (DLR), Mudchute (DLR); café.

Newham City Farm E16

King George Ave   (020) 7476 1170

This four and a half-acre farm has a wide range of livestock, including a shire horse, a donkey, cows, pigs, sheep, goats, chickens, ducks and geese. It is well geared up for casual visitors – 50,000 people pass through the gates each year. Following expansion into the neighbouring King George V Park, there is now a visitor centre. / Times: Tue-Sun 10am-5pm (4pm winter) & bank hols (closed 1pm-2pm); Tube: Royal Albert (DLR), or Plaistow (then 262 bus); in- and outdoor picnic areas.

Petticoat Lane E1

Certainly the best-known market in the East End, and possibly in London. The Sunday morning activity here is a phenomenon worth seeing whether or not you have any desire to invest in some of the low-cost clothes which are the market's speciality. / Times: Sun 9am-2pm; Tube: Liverpool Street, Aldgate.

Riverside Walk

See the introduction of the South section for suggestions of interesting walks by the Thames.

Saint Katharine's Dock E1

1–3D

St Katharine's by the Tower (as the area is more properly called) is a fine collection of buildings, principally designed by the great c19 engineer Thomas Telford, restored to make a very attractive marina. It offers by far the nicest place for a riverside stroll in central London – the Tower of London and Tower Bridge provide a dramatic backdrop. In the summer, there is lunchtime music several times a week. / www.stkaths.co.uk; Tube: Tower Hill; café.

Spitalfields Community Farm E1

Pedley St   (020) 7247 8762   1–2D

Despite its small size (one and a half-acres) and location (on former wasteground), this popular attraction manages to squeeze in most of the usual farm animals. Look out also for special events at Christmas and Easter, and during the summer, some of which are free. In addition, community members can take the National Proficiency Test Council Course (NPTC) in horticulture training for free. It begins in the spring and runs through autumn, averaging about 90 hours of training. / Times: Tue-Sun 10.30am-5pm; www.spitalfieldsfarm.htmlplanet.com; Tube: Aldgate East, Shoreditch.

Stepney Stepping Stones Farm E1

Stepney Way   (020) 7790 8204   1–2D

This eight-acre farm has all the main types of farm animals – cows, pigs, donkeys, sheep, goats, chickens, ducks and geese, as well as rabbits, guinea pigs, ferrets and chipmunks. There is also a picnic garden. The venture, now in existence for over 20 years, is run entirely by volunteers and trainees, and partly funded by the sale of produce and home cooking. Look out for events during school holidays (such as the Easter egg hunt), some of which are free. / Times: Tue-Sun 9.30am-6pm (dusk in winter); www.aboutbritain.com/steppingstonesfarm.htm; Tube: Stepney Green, Limehouse (DLR); café.

Thorndon Country Park & Hartswood, Essex

(01277) 211250 (Essex Ranger Service)

A medley of parks, lakes, woods and golf clubs makes up this rural retreat, and there's lots of history and nature to wander through, including a deer park little changed since the c16. / Times: park: 8am-dusk; Countryside Centre: summer 10am-5pm, winter Tue-Sun & bank hol 10am-3.30pm; BR: Brentwood (then 151 bus to Halfway House or 73 bus to Warley).

Tower Hamlets Cemetery Park E3

Southern Gr   (020) 8980 2373   1–2D

Built as a model necropolis for wealthy Londoners in 1841, this 27-acre site was used for burials up until 1966. A period of neglect followed, during which the local flora and fauna established themselves with a vengeance – in 1986, Tower Hamlets decided to make a virtue of necessity and declared the place a nature reserve. Some very fine Victorian tombs remain, and there is also a tree trail, which takes about 45 minutes to complete. / Times: 8.30am-dusk; Tube: Mile End.

East London

Victoria Park E3

Old Ford Rd   (020) 8985 1957   1–2D

In the 1840s, concern grew in east London about the lack of
any recreational space for the burgeoning population. Fearing
unrest, the government sold York House in Westminster to pay
for the establishment of the new Victoria Park (of 220 acres),
which is still the only large, formal park in the East End. Its
style is very much in keeping with its name – it has lakes and
fountains, one of which is a Gothic drinking fountain from
1861, large areas of bedding plants, a children's playground,
a bandstand (with live music on Sunday afternoons in July
and August) and a herd of fallow deer. Recent years have seen
much refurbishment of the facilities. The oldest model boat
club in the world meets here most Sunday mornings during
the summer. / Times: 7.30am-dusk; Tube: Bethnal Green, Mile End.

West Ham Park E7

Upton Ln   (020) 8472 3584

This 77-acre park in West Ham has been owned and run
by the Corporation of London since 1874. The recreational
facilities include a large children's playground and a seven-acre
formal garden in the south east corner of the park. During the
summer, there are children's entertainers at the bandstand,
and Sunday afternoon concerts. / Times: 7.30am-30 mins before dusk;
www.cityoflondon.gov.uk; Tube: Plaistow, Stratford.

Woolwich Free Ferry

North Woolwich Pier, New Ferry Approach   (020) 8854
8888 (Greenwich Council)

The ferry – the only free automated way to cross the Thames –
began in 1889. Paddlesteamers were, alas, replaced by the
current, less romantic, design in 1963. If you are lucky, though,
the captain might let you climb the steep steps to his eyrie.
/ Times: Mon-Sat 6.10am-8.10pm (Sat 8pm), Sun 11.30am-7.30pm;
www.members.spree.com/SIP1/freeferry; BR: north of the Thames,
North Woolwich; south of the Thames Woolwich Arsenal, Woolwich Dockyard.

Maps

MAP I – LONDON OVERVIEW

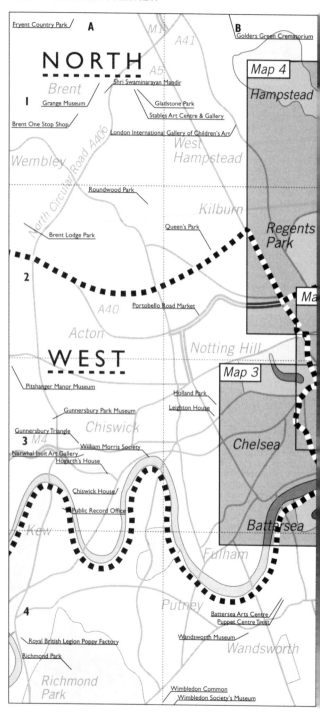

Fryent Country Park

A

B

Golders Green Crematorium

NORTH

Brent

Shri Swaminarayan Mandir

Map 4

Hampstead

I

Grange Museum

Gladstone Park

Stables Art Centre & Gallery

Brent One Stop Shop

London International Gallery of Children's Art

West Hampstead

Wembley

Roundwood Park

Kilburn

Brent Lodge Park

Queen's Park

Regents Park

2

Portobello Road Market

A40

Acton

Notting Hill

Ma

WEST

Pitshanger Manor Museum

Map 3

Holland Park

Gunnersbury Park Museum

Leighton House

Chiswick

Gunnersbury Triangle

3

Narwhal Inuit Art Gallery

William Morris Society

Hogarth's House

Chelsea

Chiswick House

Public Record Office

Kew

Battersea

Fulham

4

Putney

Battersea Arts Centre

Puppet Centre Trust

Royal British Legion Poppy Factory

Wandsworth Museum

Richmond Park

Wandsworth

Richmond Park

Wimbledon Common

Wimbledon Society's Museum

MAP I – LONDON OVERVIEW

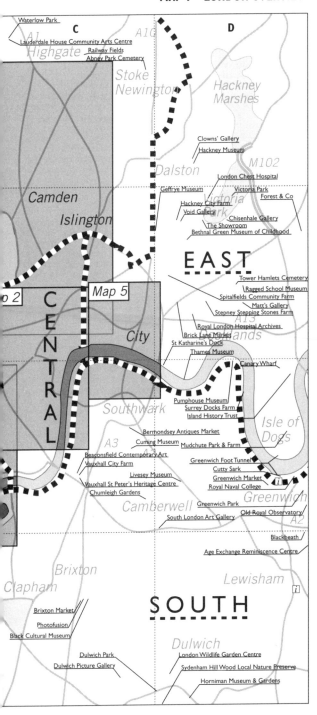

Waterlow Park
C A10 **D**
Lauderdale House Community Arts Centre
Highgate Railway Fields
Abney Park Cemetery

Stoke
Newington

Hackney
Marshes

Clowns' Gallery
Hackney Museum M102

Dalston London Chest Hospital

Camden Geffrye Museum Victoria Victoria Park Forest & Co
Islington Hackney City Farm Park
Void Gallery
Chisenhale Gallery
The Showroom
Bethnal Green Museum of Childhood

EAST

Tower Hamlets Cemetery
Ragged School Museum
Map 5 Spitalfields Community Farm
C Matt's Gallery
Stepney Stepping Stones Farm
o 2 **E** A13
N Royal London Hospital Archives
City Brick Lane Market lands
St Katharine's Dock
T Thames Museum
R Canary Wharf
A
Pumphouse Museum
L Southwark Surrey Docks Farm
Island History Trust Isle of
Dogs
Bermondsey Antiques Market
Cuming Museum Mudchute Park & Farm
Beaconsfield Contemporary Art
Vauxhall City Farm A3 Greenwich Foot Tunnel
Livesey Museum Cutty Sark
Vauxhall St Peter's Heritage Centre Greenwich Market
Chumleigh Gardens Royal Naval College
Camberwell Greenwich Park Greenwich
South London Art Gallery Old Royal Observatory
A2

Blackheath

Age Exchange Reminiscence Centre

Brixton Lewisham
Clapham

Brixton Market **SOUTH**
Photofusion
Black Cultural Museum Dulwich
Dulwich Park London Wildlife Garden Centre
Dulwich Picture Gallery Sydenham Hill Wood Local Nature Preserve
Horniman Museum & Gardens

MAP 2 – CENTRAL LONDON

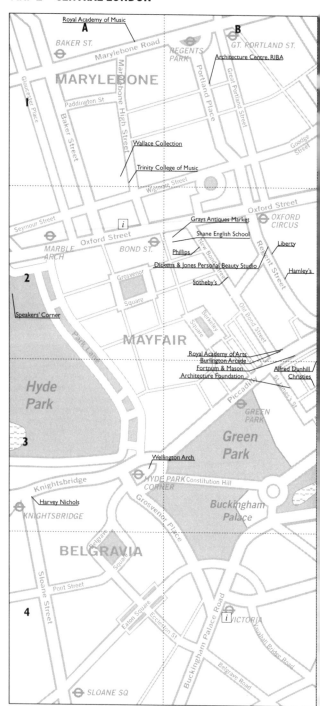

MAP 2 – CENTRAL LONDON

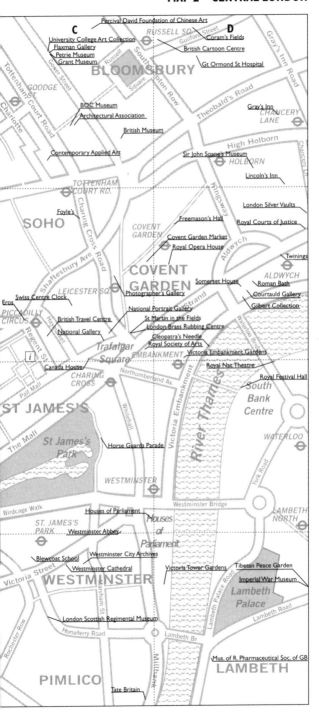

C

Percival David Foundation of Chinese Art

RUSSELL SQ.

D

University College Art Collection
Flaxman Gallery
Petrie Museum
Grant Museum

Coram's Fields
British Cartoon Centre
Gt Ormond St Hospital

BLOOMSBURY

GOODGE ST.

BOC Museum
Architectural Association

Theobald's Road

Gray's Inn

CHANCERY LANE

British Museum

High Holborn

Contemporary Applied Art

Sir John Soane's Museum
HOLBORN

Lincoln's Inn

TOTTENHAM COURT RD.

London Silver Vaults
Royal Courts of Justice

SOHO

Foyle's

COVENT GARDEN

Freemason's Hall
Covent Garden Market
Royal Opera House

Twinings

ALDWYCH

COVENT GARDEN

Somerset House
Roman Bath
Courtauld Gallery
Gilbert Collection

LEICESTER SQ.

Photographer's Gallery

Swiss Centre Clock
Eros
PICCADILLY CIRCUS

National Portrait Gallery
British Travel Centre
St Martin in the Fields
London Brass Rubbing Centre
Cleopatra's Needle
Royal Society of Arts

National Gallery

Trafalgar Square

EMBANKMENT

Victoria Embankment Gardens

Canada House

CHARING CROSS

Northumberland Av.

Royal Nat Theatre

Royal Festival Hall

ST JAMES'S

The Mall

St James's Park

Horse Guards Parade

South Bank Centre

WATERLOO

WESTMINSTER

River Thames

Birdcage Walk

ST. JAMES'S PARK

Houses of Parliament

Westminster Abbey

Houses of Parliament

Westminster Bridge

LAMBETH NORTH

Blewcoat School
Westminster City Archives
Westminster Cathedral

WESTMINSTER

Victoria Tower Gardens

Tibetan Peace Garden
Imperial War Museum

Lambeth Palace

Victoria Street

London Scottish Regimental Museum

Horseferry Road

Lambeth Br

Lambeth Palace Road

Lambeth Road

PIMLICO

Tate Britain

Mus. of R. Pharmaceutical Soc. of GB

LAMBETH

MAP 3 – WEST LONDON (SW POSTCODES)

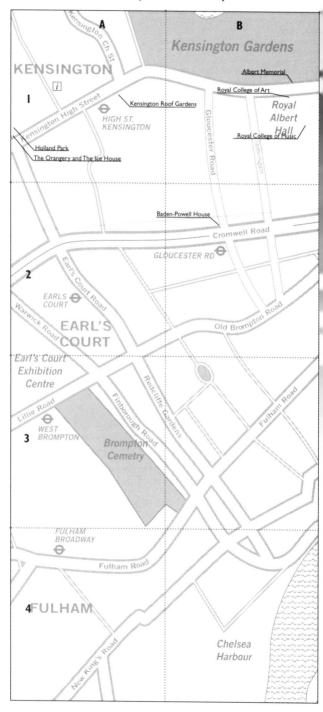

MAP 3 – WEST LONDON (SW POSTCODES)

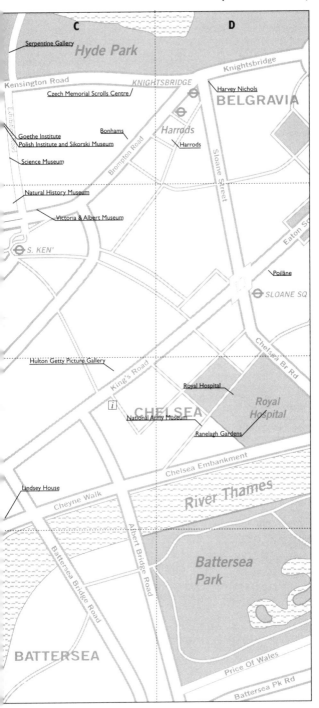

MAP 4 – NORTH LONDON

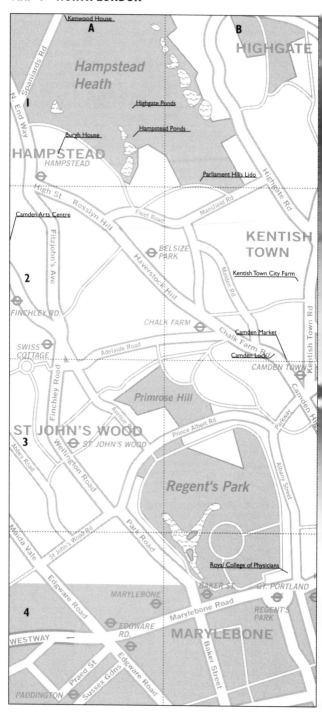

MAP 4 – NORTH LONGON

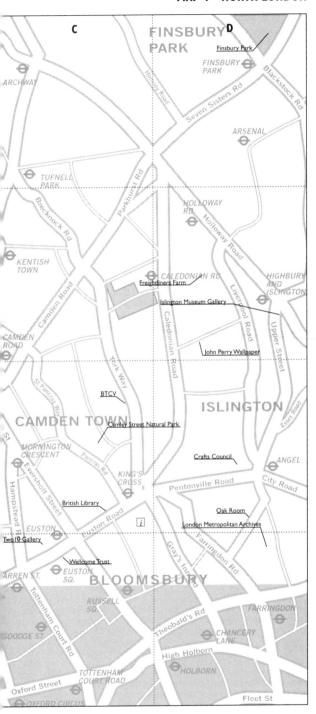

C

D

FINSBURY
PARK

Finsbury Park

FINSBURY
PARK

Blackstock Rd

ARCHWAY

Hornsey Road

Seven Sisters Rd

ARSENAL

TUFNELL
PARK

Parkhurst Rd

HOLLOWAY
RD.

Holloway Road

Breckneck Rd

KENTISH
TOWN

Camden Road

CALEDONIAN RD.

Freightliners Farm

HIGHBURY
AND
ISLINGTON

Liverpool Road

Upper Street

Islington Museum Gallery

CAMDEN
ROAD

Caledonian Road

John Perry Wallpaper

York Way

St Pancras Way

BTCV

ISLINGTON

Essex Road

CAMDEN TOWN

Camley Street Natural Park

MORNINGTON
CRESCENT

Pancras Rd

Crafts Council

ANGEL

Eversholt Street

KING'S
CROSS

Pentonville Road

City Road

Hampstead Rd

British Library

Euston Road

[i]

Oak Room

London Metropolitan Archives

Farringdon Rd

EUSTON

Two10 Gallery

Wellcome Trust

ARREN ST.

EUSTON
SQ.

BLOOMSBURY

Gray's Inn Rd

RUSSELL
SQ.

FARRINGDON

Tottenham Court Rd

Theobald's Rd

GOODGE ST.

CHANCERY
LANE

High Holborn

HOLBORN

TOTTENHAM
COURT ROAD

Oxford Street

OXFORD CIRCUS

Fleet St

MAP 5 – THE CITY

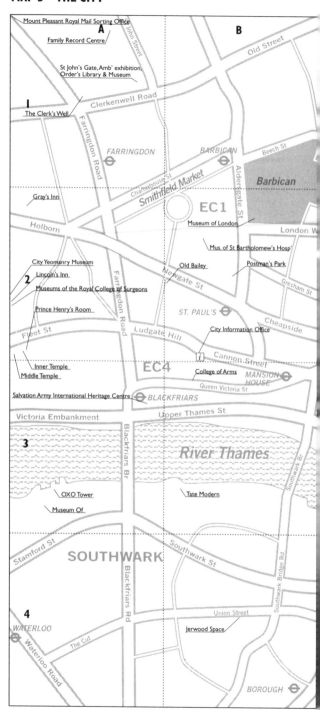

Mount Pleasant Royal Mail Sorting Office

Family Record Centre

St John's Gate, Amb' exhibition, Order's Library & Museum

A

B

John Street

Old Street

Clerkenwell Road

I

The Clerk's Well

FARRINGDON

Farringdon Road

Charterhouse St

Smithfield Market

BARBICAN

Beech St

Aldersgate St

Barbican

Gray's Inn

Holborn

EC1

Museum of London

London W

Mus. of St Bartholomew's Hosp'

City Yeomanry Museum

Lincoln's Inn

Museums of the Royal College of Surgeons

Prince Henry's Room

2

Farringdon Road

Old Bailey

Newgate St

Postman's Park

Gresham St

ST. PAUL'S

Cheapside

Fleet St

Ludgate Hill

City Information Office

Inner Temple

Middle Temple

EC4

Cannon Street

College of Arms

MANSION HOUSE

Queen Victoria St

Salvation Army International Heritage Centre

BLACKFRIARS

Victoria Embankment

Upper Thames St

3

Blackfriars Br

River Thames

Southwark Br

OXO Tower

Tate Modern

Museum Of

Stamford St

SOUTHWARK

Southwark St

Blackfriars Rd

Southwark Bridge Rd

4

WATERLOO

Union Street

Jerwood Space

Waterloo Road

The Cut

BOROUGH

MAP 5 – THE CITY

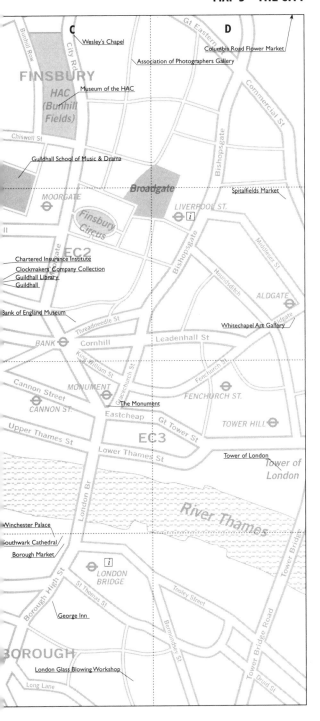

C

Wesley's Chapel

Columbia Road Flower Market

Association of Photographers Gallery

FINSBURY

HAC
(Bunhill
Fields)

Museum of the HAC

Chiswell St

Guildhall School of Music & Drama

MOORGATE

Broadgate

LIVERPOOL ST.

Spitalfields Market

Finsbury
Circus

EC2

Chartered Insurance Institute
Clockmakers' Company Collection
Guildhall Library
Guildhall

Bank of England Museum

ALDGATE

Whitechapel Art Gallery

Threadneedle St

BANK   Cornhill

Leadenhall St

King William St

MONUMENT

FENCHURCH ST.

Cannon Street

CANNON ST.

The Monument

Eastcheap   Gt Tower St

TOWER HILL

Upper Thames St

EC3

Lower Thames St

Tower of London

Tower of
London

London Br

River Thames

Winchester Palace

Southwark Cathedral

Borough Market

LONDON
BRIDGE

St Thomas St

Tooley Street

George Inn

BOROUGH

London Glass Blowing Workshop

Long Lane

D

Gt Eastern

Commercial St

Bishopsgate

Bishopsgate

Middlesex St

Houndsditch

Fenchurch St

Tower Bridge

Tower Bridge Road

Bermondsey St

Druid St

Indexes

Index by type of attraction

Index by type of attraction

Alphabetical index

Alphabetical index